The Maltese Bodkin

by

David Belke

SAMUEL FRENCH

FOUNDED 1830

NEW YORK HOLLYWOOD LONDON TORONTO

SAMUELFRENCH.COM

ISBN 978-0-573-65245-5   Printed in U.S.A.   #14835

IMPORTANT BILLING AND CREDIT REQUIREMENTS

All producers of *THE MALTESE BODKIN* must give credit to the Author of the Play in all programs distributed in connection with performances of the Play, and in all instances in which the title of the Play appears for the purposes of advertising, publicizing or otherwise exploiting the Play and/or a production. The name of the Author *must* appear on a separate line on which no other name appears, immediately following the title and *must* appear in size of type not less than fifty percent of the size of the title type.

THE MALTESE BODKIN was originally produced by The ACME Theatre Company at the 1991 Edmonton Fringe Theatre Festival. The production was designed by David Belke with fight choreography by Anton Solomon and musical direction by Bill Damur, stage management by Kristina Schwager and graphic design by Chris Belke. The production was under the direction of Patti Stiles, with the following cast and musicians:

BIRNAM WOOD . . . . William Davidson

VIOLA . . . . Kate Twa

CHARLOTTE, MISTRESS QUICKLY . . . . Michale Ascher

ANTONIO, MERCUTIO, PUCK,

RICHARD, ROSENCRANTZ . . . . .Michael Charrois

IAGO, RATCLIFFE, DONALBAIN,

GUILDENSTERN, SEBASTIAN . . . . Nathan Fillion

FALSTAFF, CATESBY, FANG, PROSPERO . . . . Glenn Nelson

Lute and string instruments performed by Bill Damur

Saxophone and other wind instruments performed by Chris Helman

The revised version of *THE MALTESE BODKIN* was produced by The ACME Theatre Company in 1995 at the Varscona Theatre in Edmonton, Alberta. The production was designed by David Belke with fight choreography by Raul Tome and musical direction by Bill Damur, stage management by Shaeh Fialkow and graphic design by Chris Belke. The production was under the direction of John Hudson, with the following cast and musicians:

BIRNAM WOOD . . . . John Sproule

VIOLA . . . . Coralie Cairns

CHARLOTTE, MISTRESS QUICKLY . . . . Sarah Gale

ANTONIO, MERCUTIO, PUCK,

RICHARD, ROSENCRANTZ . . . . Michael Charrois

IAGO, RATCLIFFE, DONALBAIN,

GUILDENSTERN, SEBASTIAN . . . . Mark Meer

FALSTAFF, CATESBY, FANG, PROSPERO . . . . Ashley Wright

Lute and string instruments performed by Bill Damur

Saxophone and other wind instruments performed by
Rosemarie Seaver

CAST

BIRNAM WOOD — Dan		a private investigator
CHARLOTTE — Lauren		Wood's receptionist and secretary
ANTONIO — Kate K		a merchant of Venice
VIOLA DA MESSALINE — Jonelle		a mysterious client
IAGO — Greg		a sword for hire and villain
MISTRESS NELL QUICKLY – Mel		proprietress of the Boar's Head Tavern
SIR JOHN FALSTAFF — Dave		rogue, wit and information source
MERCUTIO OF VERONA — Esther		a man on a quest
SIR RICHARD RATCLIFFE — Samantha		a thug
SIR WILLIAM CATESBY — Geoff		a dangerous thug
PUCK — Hannah		a fairy trickster
DONALBAIN — Steven		former prince of Scotland
SERGEANT FANG — Emily		a constable
PROSPERO — Renee		Duke of Milan and sorcerer
RICHARD, DUKE OF GLOUCESTER— Eric		an evil mastermind
ROSENCRANTZ and GUILDENSTERN		Danes in danger
SEBASTIAN — Seth — Kate McD.		a missing person
Chelsea		

SCENES

Act One

Act Two

PRODUCTION NOTES

CASTING: Although this play can be performed with casting each character with an individual actor, it was written to be performed by six. In this case the only characters exclusively played by a single actor are Wood and Viola. The rest of the casting broke down this way:

Actor 1: Antonio, Mercutio, Puck, Richard, Rosencrantz

Actor 2: Charlotte, Quickly

Actor 3: Iago, Ratcliffe, Donalbain, Guildenstern, Sebastian

Actor 4: Falstaff, Catesby, Fang, Prospero

PLAYING PUCK: Although there many ways of portraying the fairy trickster, the original production featured a very successful and simple illusion. The "Little Man" illusion is achieved by having the actor playing the character put his hands in shoes or boots playing the character's feet. With the aid a specially prepared jacket, a second actor (in this case the actor playing Charlotte) comes from behind and extends their arms around the first actor to play the character's arms and hands. The two actors' bodies are hidden with black drapery. This creates a truly elfin figure capable of not only a full range of acting ability, but also the ability to float and fly.

MUSIC: In the original production we found live music to be highly successful in evoking the play's atmosphere. The premiere production featured a musical duo, one playing saxophone and the other playing lute and other Renaissance string instruments. Their on stage costumes reflected the historic periods of their instruments.

ACCENT: As in Shakespearean punctuation the accented syllable (é) indicates a stressed pronunciation, not a French one.

Day1

ACT ONE

Scene One

(*In darkness to begin. A dim light resolves itself on a solitary figure as a lonely saxophone wails in the background. The figure is a man dressed in a trench coat and fedora. A cigarette in his mouth, he flicks a lighter which briefly illuminates his face. This is* **BIRNAM WOOD**, *private investigator. Between scenes the character serves as a narrator through his monologues and will always come back to the same position and light in order to resume his narrative role. He moves to light his cigarette, but pauses and regards the flame.*)

WOOD. O for a muse of fire… (*he extinguishes the flame, he addresses the audience*) The world's a lousy place sometimes, and sometimes the worst thing about it can be the place you find yourself in. Like I never wanted to find myself in London. Especially not in 1605. Lousy year. Lousy town. Mud caked, poverty stricken, tumble down old dive. With the best kept lawns in all the world. Wasn't my kind of town. Too snooty. Too foggy. Too… Jacobean.

But you gotta make do with where you're at and running the P.I. game with Archie Heath was one of the few good things that happened to me since I got there. Archie was a good egg. Maybe a little too soft-boiled for his own good, but he was the best pal I ever had. The street word was my job. Business was good. Maybe too good.

The noble houses always had need of a smart snoop who could keep his mouth shut. The King especially. That's how I ended up out of the country when the spit hit the fan. And when I got back, there was a pile of

unfinished reports, the office was a mess and Archie…
My partner Archie Heath was dead.

(*With a musical bridge and cross fade we arrive in
Wood's office.*

*It is evening. The scene is a typical 1940's style detec-
tive's office. Large wooden desk with accompanying
swivel chair. There is a utilitarian old chair for clients in
front of the desk. A metal file cabinet and coat tree in the
corner. A general disorder of papers, empty bottles and
other neglected articles have taken possession of every
surface. On the desk is a name plate reading "B. Wood."
A window with blinds overlooks the Thames and Jacobean London. A door connecting to the outer office and
reception area bears a frosted glass pane with the reversed
inscription: "Wood & Heath."*

WOOD *lies in a drunken collapse behind the desk. There
is a long moment of stillness.*

There is the sound of soft movement and then
CHARLOTTE *cautiously enters. She is a reasonably
attractive woman in her mid-thirties dressed in a fashion
appropriate for the golden age of detectives. Both she and
the dress have seen better days. Her jewelry is perhaps
a little garish, her make-up perhaps a little thick, but
beneath it all is a sincere and caring woman.*

*Carrying the office mail, she looks with concern at her
boss. She opens her mouth to speak, then pauses. Careful
not to make a sound she approaches* **WOOD** *sprawled on
his desk. With more care than is required she drops the
mail on his desk. She pauses for a moment, hoping to
be noticed. But receiving no sign from her employer she
begins to leave. Before she has exited though, she stops
again and finally having made up her mind, speaks.
With a Brooklyn accent.*)

CHARLOTTE. Bernie? (*she takes the bottle from Wood's limp
hand, sniffs it and sets it on the desk*) Bernie? (*making a
quick attempt at organizing the area*) He's waiting for you
in the office. He wants to hire you. A new case is just
what you need.

WOOD (*not moving*) I ain't seeing no one, Charlotte.

CHARLOTTE. Bernie, this isn't right. It's been a week since you came back and you ain't left the office since you heard about... Bernie, there wasn't nothin' you coulda done if you'd have been here. You know that. At least you used to. But we need the work. Look at the bills –

WOOD. They found the guy that done it yet?

CHARLOTTE. No.

WOOD. The murder weapon?

CHARLOTTE. No.

WOOD. Then send him away.

CHARLOTTE. Boss...

WOOD. Hasn't anyone in this limey pesthole ever heard of a period of mourning? Send him away.

(CHARLOTTE *reluctantly leaves.* WOOD *slumps behind his desk. Silence. Then softly at first, shouting from the outer office. A man bursts into the office. He is dressed in the fashion of a Renaissance nobleman: velvet doublet, cloak and breeches. A purse of gold hangs from his belt. This is* ANTONIO, *the merchant of Venice and he is in a foul mood. He is closely followed by* CHARLOTTE *trying to restrain him.*)

ANTONIO (*seeing* WOOD) You!

CHARLOTTE. I'm sorry, boss. He got away from me.

ANTONIO. Mr. Wood. I have for a fortnight been waiting to see you.

WOOD. Well, you're seeing me.

ANTONIO. Sirrah, my life is in danger.

WOOD. I'm not taking work.

ANTONIO (*indicating his purse*) I am willing to pay well for your services.

CHARLOTTE. You could just listen to him. You don't have to take the job or nothin'.

WOOD (*considers, then*) Beat it, Mom.

(CHARLOTTE *exits with a smile.* WOOD *turns his attention to* ANTONIO.)

WOOD. Okay. What's your story, Mister...?

ANTONIO. My name is Antonio. I am a merchant of Venice.

WOOD. Birnam Wood, detective to the stars. So what's the story?

ANTONIO. I have been threatened.

WOOD. Haven't we all?

ANTONIO. I am in fear of injury.

WOOD. Who's after you?

ANTONIO. A heathen usurer.

WOOD. A loan shark? A lousy loan shark?

ANTONIO. I am in fear, sir, for life and limb. Due to a reversal of fortunes I was required to borrow a sum of gold from a roguish usurer.

WOOD. You don't need an investigator. You need an accountant.

ANTONIO. I require a strong arm. To force the poltroon to renounce his claim. If thou wilt apply... persuasive measures upon my oppressor, thou wilt be admirably compensated for thy efforts on my behalf.

WOOD. Beat it.

ANTONIO. Pardon?

WOOD. Scram. I ain't no cheap thug.

ANTONIO. Oh, if 'tis greater reward thou desirest...

WOOD. That does it.

(**WOOD** *gives* **ANTONIO** *the bum's rush.*)

ANTONIO. But he demands a pound of my flesh!

WOOD. Make sure he takes it from your head. You'll never miss it.

ANTONIO. I am a citizen of Venice. I will speak to our soldiers.

WOOD. That's right. Tell it to the marines.

(*He throws* **ANTONIO** *out of his office and slams the door on him.*)

ANTONIO (*from the other side*) You'll be hearing from my lawyer!

WOOD. Friggin' middle class. Never know their place.

(**WOOD** *returns to his chair, picks up an empty bottle and tries to take a swig. There is a knock on the door and* **CHARLOTTE** *tentatively sticks her head into the office.*)

CHARLOTTE. Boss?

WOOD. I never want to see another Venetian. Understand?

CHARLOTTE. Sorry, boss. (*beat*) Ah, listen. There's someone else in the office...

WOOD. I won't see 'im.

CHARLOTTE. I think maybe you should. She's a client.

WOOD. I ain't takin' clients.

CHARLOTTE. She isn't askin' to be a client. She *is* a client. She was the person who hired Mr. Heath when he... (**WOOD** *turns in his chair and intently regards* **CHARLOTTE**) She came to see Mr. Heath. (*beat*) She ain't Venetian, boss.

WOOD. Okay. Show her in.

(**CHARLOTTE** *exits.* **WOOD** *is just pulling on his jacket when the client enters and stands framed in the doorway. She is a dark, sultry woman dressed in an elaborate Elizabethan gown. There is a suggestion of wealth about her and she definitely projects an atmosphere of poise and icy calculation. She is beautiful. This is* **VIOLA.**)

VIOLA (*studying him*) Thou art not the man I expected.

WOOD. Sorry to disappoint you.

VIOLA. 'Tis not disappointment of which I speak, only expectation of another. 'Twas Mr. Heath whom I employed in my search to find my... By Helen, I speak too dear, too much to thee bequeath. I must speak to he who serveth me, please you, summon Mr. Heath.

WOOD. That might be a little difficult, Miss...

VIOLA. I am called Viola da Messaline, daughter of a noble merchant clan but newly arrived to thy shores. But prithee, tell me man, where is he I hired?

WOOD. You can talk to me.

VIOLA. Thou?

WOOD. I'm his partner.

VIOLA. And fellow in arms?

WOOD. I guess.

VIOLA. And Mr. Heath?

WOOD. Archie… Archie's dead.

VIOLA. 'Tis true. I know. Please forgive a solitary's false and desperate deed. But I had to know if thou were, sir, the man I truly need.

WOOD. Is that a habit of yours? Testing everyone you meet?

VIOLA. Only those who would labor on my behalf, Mr. Wood.

WOOD. Hm. I ain't working for you.

VIOLA. But thou must. If thou wilt not put shoulder to Archie's task, then who shall be my champion? Look to thy heart. 'Tis a matter of grave family consequence and one of deadly deep concern.

WOOD. I'll think about it. But I'll need some answers first.

VIOLA. Thou art a good and Christian knight, Sir Wood. I shall respondeth as I should.

WOOD. What was the case Archie was working on?

VIOLA. Did he not inform thee?

WOOD. I was out of town.

VIOLA. Indeed? Where?

WOOD. I'm asking the questions.

VIOLA. Thou wert where?

WOOD. In Denmark. On an errand for a client.

VIOLA. Tell me who.

WOOD. What was the case Archie was working on?

VIOLA. I search, sir, for my brother. My family's home is the isle of fairest Messaline. Pure, bounteous isle. Our father was a fair and honorable merchant who traded from the distant Indes to far silken shores. He hath but recently passed to Heaven's bosom and mine Uncle, by virtue of his seniority, did rise to take my father's place.

Belike the covetous packrat did mine Uncle gather to his grasp both mine and my brother's inheritance. And such was his enmity that we were decided to find our fortunes elsewhere. As my father had comrades in the ways of trade on Britain's rocky shores, so we set out: myself, my brother and what goods we could to this new minted nation.

WOOD. What happened?

VIOLA. The ocean voyage was peaceful 'Tis true, but 'pon entry to thy stormy channel the argosy was tempest tost, the ship washed upon the Kentish coast and my brother... Nowhere to be found. 'Twas fortunate that I survived the disaster with my assets intact and directly began my search for my brother as is my sisterly obligation.

WOOD. Why look in London? We're miles from the Channel.

VIOLA. 'Twas always our mutual wish to settle in London's gentle climes.

WOOD. And this was the case Archie was working on?

VIOLA. In faith, Archie –

WOOD. Archie?

VIOLA. Excuse, Mr. Heath seemed so eager to help. Art thou eager to help, Mr. Wood?

WOOD. What was your brother's name?

VIOLA. Then thou shall undertake my venture. My brother Sebastian is called. He is but one score year. A man fair of countenance and carriage.

WOOD. Do you have any idea where Archie went to look for the kid?

VIOLA. Mr. Heath spoke of searching the merchant houses. In sooth if Sebastian's resources survived as mine did, he may have found sanctuary in any London port.

WOOD. London's a big city, Miss da...

VIOLA. Messaline.

WOOD. Right.

VIOLA. One might also try searching the noble houses. Sebastian was… is an ingratiatory.

WOOD. What else do you know about Archie's investigation?

VIOLA. I told thee all I know.

WOOD. Did he have any theories?

VIOLA. Faith sir, I know not.

WOOD. You don't know who his contacts were?

VIOLA. Nay, I do not.

WOOD. He mention any names?

VIOLA. Nay, he did not.

WOOD. Anybody get mad at him?

VIOLA. I know not.

WOOD. Mad enough to kill him?

VIOLA. I DON'T KNOW! (*pause*) I beg your pardon, Mr. Wood. I am unaccustomed to being treated in a such a manner. Shall we return to the task at hand? By what rate shall I pay thee for thy services?

WOOD. I ain't taking the case.

VIOLA. But I thought *— there is no finding*

WOOD. All I care about is my partner. He died working for you. I thought I might find out why or how. You don't know nothin'.

VIOLA. I know he died when stabbed through the back.

WOOD. That's old news.

VIOLA. I know where the murder weapon is.

WOOD. Where?

VIOLA. I shall fetch it for thee, if in return thou wilt promise to search for my brother.

WOOD. No deals. You're withholding evidence. I'll have you up on charges.

VIOLA. I will deny all. Will the courts arrest me on thy testimony alone? The law hath little love for thee, Mr. Wood. So. Is our bargain sealed? I tell thee of the knife's hiding place and thy services are mine.

WOOD. Thirty five pounds a day plus expenses.

VIOLA. You've sold yourself short, Mr. Wood.

WOOD. Where's the weapon?

(*With a smile* **VIOLA** *produces from her bosom the jeweled dagger which was hidden there suspended from a gold chain. She presses it into* **WOOD**'s *hand.*)

WOOD. Where did you get it?

VIOLA. From the bloodied back of Mr. Heath. 'Twas meeting me he was embarked when he was so cruelly struck. I found the body in the alleyway and took the knife.

WOOD (*examines the knife*) Spanish steel. High quality. Lousy weight and balance. What's on the blade? A cross?

VIOLA. The cross of Malta.

WOOD. A Maltese Bodkin. But how did it end up so far from home? And more importantly how did it end up in my partner's back?

VIOLA. The answers are thy concern. As Sebastian's finding as mine own.

WOOD. I'll call you when I have some information. Goodbye, Miss da…

VIOLA. Da Messaline.

WOOD. Yeah.

VIOLA. I stay at the Dolphin. You can find me in room three. I shall await thy summons. (moves to the door) I am so glad thou hast taken on the case. I know thou wilt find my brother. I have such confidence in thee.

(**VIOLA** *exits.* **WOOD** *continues to examine the knife.* **CHARLOTTE** *enters.*)

CHARLOTTE. So. Did you take the case?

WOOD. She cleaned it.

CHARLOTTE. What?

WOOD. She took the knife out of Archie's body and she cleaned it.

CHARLOTTE. She's a cool one.

WOOD. What do you think of her?

CHARLOTTE. She's a thinker. A smart one. She'll pay her bills on time. Pretty fancy knife.

WOOD. Expensive. We need some checking around the court. I want you to find Donalbain. He owes us a few favors. He's still a guest of the King ain't he?

CHARLOTTE. Yeah. For the last three years, the freeloader.

WOOD. This time of day he'll probably be at the Queen's Head. Tell him to meet me here tomorrow morning.

CHARLOTTE. Check. And what'll you be doin'?

WOOD. Going through our weapons files. See if this thing's been reported missing. Then I'll dig through Archie's files. See if there's some clue as to what he was up to we might have missed before.

CHARLOTTE. Right. (*turns to go, pauses at the door*) It's good to see you up on your feet again, Bernie.

WOOD. Go.

(**CHARLOTTE** *exits leaving* **WOOD** *alone still pondering the knife. Finally he places the dagger in a desk drawer. He turns to the file cabinet behind the desk and opens a drawer to examine files. His back is to the office door, so he is unaware as it slowly opens. Slipping into the room is a ferrety little man with a sharp anticipatory expression. He is dressed in the worn leather clothing of a soldier and a sword and dagger hang from his belt. Seeing* **WOOD**'s *back to him, the man quietly and gleefully draws his knife. He silently advances toward* **WOOD**. *As soon as he is within striking distance he raises his weapon. But* **WOOD** *suddenly turns and is revealed with a pistol in his hand pointed directly at the intruder, whose name is* **IAGO**.)

WOOD. Is that any way to enter a room?

IAGO (*thick Italian accent*) Your door was open. I came in. I put away the knife. 'Twas a test merely of your reputation. It is intact.

WOOD. My reputation or my back?

IAGO. Both, luckily.

WOOD. Sit down where I can keep an eye on you.

IAGO. You have nothing to fear, merciful sir. I am but a messenger from one greater than I.

WOOD. And just who might that be?

IAGO. Someone who wishes for the moment to cloak himself in anon... anon... He does not wish you to know who he is. (*pause*) You had visitor. A woman was here. I saw her enter. I saw her go. A radiant vision, I thought.

WOOD. Why're you following the lady?

IAGO. She is thought to be in possession of a certain item of which my employer is desirous. Assigned the task of following the woman, I follow her. A not entirely unpleasant task to be certain.

WOOD. All right, cut the malarkey and answer my question. Who are you?

IAGO. I am but a recent arrival to these shores. I was at one time a soldier, but circumstances forced me to make a hasty departure from that position. My name is Iago, formerly of Venice.

WOOD. Another friggin' Venetian.

IAGO. May I ask you a question, oh noble and powerful sir?

WOOD. Flattery will get you nowhere.

IAGO. That's what you think. I am curious. What did the woman want?

WOOD. Why?

IAGO. I care not. 'Tis my master who wishes to know. He is a brave and noble patrician who has it within his means to reward well those who serve him. Or help him. The woman is...?

WOOD. Your boss is...?

IAGO. Alas, anon... anon... anony... I cannot say. What did the woman see you for?

WOOD. What do you think she wanted?

IAGO. I assume nothing. A lovers' tryst perhaps? But no. You are too clever for that. She is of great danger that woman. As are all women by degrees. Trust her not.

WOOD. And why should I trust you?

IAGO. Have I not been honest with thee? My employer desires of me a duty. Tell me. Have you seen a bejeweled bodkin of such a length? It is made of the finest steel and bears the cross of Malta upon the blade.

WOOD. Never seen it.

IAGO. That is a shame. My noble master is willing to reward greatly the finder of this blade a great treasure.

WOOD. And that is...?

IAGO. His life.

WOOD. Is that a threat?

IAGO. Nay, sir. How could I think to offer threat to such a noble countenance as yourself?

WOOD. Ever hear of a guy named Archie Heath?

IAGO. He is your partner is he not? And dead too, poor man.

WOOD. You know how he died?

IAGO. I know but what my employer informs me.

WOOD. And what's that?

IAGO. Not to tell what I know.

WOOD (*slaps* **IAGO**) No?

IAGO. I cannot say.

WOOD (*slaps again*) Say what?

IAGO. I cannot say what I know or say what I knew, only say what I said when I said it to you.

WOOD. Beat it. And if I ever see you again...

IAGO. You shall not see me, sirrah. Unless your purposes cross those of my employer. Then I shall be the last thing you ever see.

(**IAGO** *quickly exits.* **WOOD** *dashes after him, gun at the ready, By the time he reaches the door and looks out into the outer office* **IAGO** *has vanished.* **WOOD** *holsters his gun. The saxophone music plays under as* **WOOD** *grabs his trench coat and hat and launches himself out of the office into the night.*)

(*FADE OUT*)

Scene Two

WOOD (*addressing audience*) There are guys who'll tell you they got life all figured out. That it's all a matter of bein' or not bein'. Me, I try not to think about stuff like that. For a week I sat in the office tryin' to get a handle on Archie's case. And then in less than half an hour I had a client, a case and a murder weapon. I'd started with less before. But I still needed help and information. And luckily I could get both. In East-cheap. In the Boar's Head Tavern.

(*The saxophone wails as* **WOOD** *moves into the Boar's Head Tavern and it is soon overwhelmed by the sounds of carousing patrons and drunken singing. The tavern is darkly lit by candlelit, but it is a warm, homey place despite the roughhewn walls and furniture.* **MISTRESS NELL QUICKLY** *is behind the bar cheerfully yelling abuse in a vain attempt to keep order amongst her customers. She is a harried, but bighearted woman well versed in dealing with all classes of people be they drunk or sober. She is in late middle age but possesses the vigor of a woman half her age.*

WOOD *enters and proceeds to the bar to confer with* **QUICKLY**. *Shortly after, a well dressed stranger armed with a dueling sword follows. He finds himself a seat at a table well situated to keep* **WOOD** *under observation.*)

QUICKLY. Cor! Will you look what the wind blew in. Come in from the cold you cold blooded savage and order yourself a pint.

WOOD. Like to Nell, but I'm here on business.

QUICKLY. First time I sees you in days and it's business. You sure know how to break an old woman's heart, Woody.

WOOD. I couldn't do that, Nell. Even if I wanted to. How are our guests?

QUICKLY. Ah, they're fine. I make sure they're well fed and warm and safe from pryin' eyes. They're like the

Mel - better with the movement

children I never, you know. Truth to tell, they're happy to be breathin.' Lucky they are, if what you told me is true.

WOOD. It is.

QUICKLY. So this is a job for the King? I never thought. And all the way from Denmark they are? Never saw a Denmarker in London 'fore. Strange times we're livin' in.

WOOD. You should see how strange things look from my side. Is the Fat Man around?

QUICKLY. That wine sodden old leech? What want you with him?

WOOD. I need to talk.

QUICKLY. Aye, and a fine one for talkin' he is. Faith, but he loves to keep a gale blowin' through his lips. Only time he stops is when he's pourin' a keg of my finest down his throat.

WOOD. Is he here?

QUICKLY. So long as the taps are flowing and the barrels have still the dew of Burgundy 'pon their staves. Sir John! Jack, you old parasite! You have a visitor!

FALSTAFF (*unseen*) Now, Hal, what time of day is it, lad?

QUICKLY. Rouse yourself, you overfilled wineskin. 'Tis not Hal who seeks thee, but our man Wood.

FALSTAFF (*pulling himself up from behind the bar*) Man? Wood? A man would do much, but only when properly fortified. Another round, Mistress.

WOOD. Sir John Falstaff. Still drinking yourself under the table I see.

FALSTAFF. God in heaven! Can this be Birnam Wood raised himself from his tomb at last? Come Mistress, another round for Lazarus and another for I, his prophet.

QUICKLY. You've had too much already, Sir Jack. You've drained the cask.

FALSTAFF. I am like the ocean, good Mistress. Spill what you may into in me, but the tide takes it away and calls for more. Come, let's have a second flood to wash this poor sinner away.

WOOD. I always said you were all wet.

FALSTAFF. Wet without would wet within, Wood. (*he laughs in* WOOD*'s face*)

WOOD. Ah, Sir John. The sweet smell of excess. Pour us a round, Nell. And pour one for yourself.

QUICKLY. And who am I to turn down such a gentlemanly request? (*she pours drinks*)

FALSTAFF. Ah now, there is a sight to raise men's spirits, if only in anticipation of raiséd cups. Very well then. I propose a toast in memory of fallen comrades. Our very own Archie Heath.

WOOD. All right then. To Archie Heath. (*brings the cup to his lips, but* FALSTAFF *stops him*)

FALSTAFF. By Jupiter and all his kin! That is no manner by which to eulogize a comrade. Listen unto me. (*thinks for moment and then raises his cup*) We raise a jar in memory of Archie Heath. Like Apollo in aspect, like unto the Wanderer in craft. A comfort to the ladies and well remembered financier of many a circle of port at the Boar's Head here. In honor of thee, dear friend, shall every glass be dry. (**FALSTAFF, WOOD** *and* **QUICKLY** *drain their glasses*) And that is how the fallen are raised and rememberéd.

WOOD. Pour him another. Nell.

FALSTAFF. Ah, thou art a boon, Wood. But now, what is thy suit? And why is it so badly tailored?

WOOD. Have you found anything out about Archie?

FALSTAFF. Am I not Sir John Falstaff? A very honorable knight? And men and women oft times say things in the midst of nights that they care not to remember 'pon the morn. And as I am a silent knight if not a holy knight then do I listen. I have heard things, dear sir-

WOOD. Jack! Any word about Archie?

FALSTAFF. I have news, good sir, but o'er cautious am I with Mistress Quickly hovering so near. Can we not set her a task to occupy her attention while we confer? Perhaps she might draw a draught to distract her attention while we speak?

WOOD. Draw him an ale, Nell. It's on me.

QUICKLY. On you, but soon it shall be down him.

FALSTAFF. Where the draught shall be happy amidst so many of brothers.

> (**QUICKLY** *exits.* **WOOD** *and* **FALSTAFF**, *intent on conversation, do not see the entrance of* **RATCLIFFE**, *a silent but deadly thug. He is armed with a sword and wears a hooded cloak to hide his identity. The Stranger who followed* **WOOD** *in has however noted the new danger and splits his attention between* **RATCLIFFE** *and* **WOOD**.)

WOOD. What've you heard?

FALSTAFF. 'Tis strange, my friend. At the Lupper's Head naught is said of our demiséd friend. Nor at the Rose and Crown or the Ship's Bell or the King's Head or the Queen's Head for that matter. Though through sense of duty I enforced myself a visit to every tavern in Eastcheap I heard not a word. And some I forced myself a second call. And a third. The fourth visits were made out of obligation only.

WOOD. I thought you said you found something.

FALSTAFF. A nothing that is something, my friend. It is impossible to be such a crime committed by a rogue that he does not brag of it. And yet no word is said. I fear no petty criminal slew our poor, blasted Heath.

WOOD. Then it was a pro job?

FALSTAFF. Or a noble's errand. One way or t'other 'tis a dangerous turn to the affair. What was it that dear Archie was laboring on when he fell to such fell purpose?

WOOD. A family matter. Lookin' for some dame's brother. I got the case now.

FALSTAFF. Make certain you do not receive poor Archie's payment. Still 'tis good to see thee friend Wood. Thou hast brooded too deeply in this matter. Such dismal thoughts are poisonous to one's digestion and thus I do in fact avoid them.

WOOD. Like you avoid so many other things. Work. Exercise..

FALSTAFF. I have placed two times twenty years of care and affection in the tender care of mine appetites. (*patting his stomach*) Grown a better man for it. (**QUICKLY** *enters with two full mugs of ale*) Ah, Mistress Quickly with fair companions.

QUICKLY. All the way from the cellar.

FALSTAFF. Long time coming and half to go. (*he drains the stein*) A fair payment.

WOOD. Do either of you know anything about knives?

FALSTAFF. Only that they cut and you hold the point away from yourself.

QUICKLY. Any special knife?

WOOD. Small. Light. About this long. Jewels on the handle. There's a Maltese cross cut into the blade.

(*Both the Stranger and* **RATCLIFFE** *suddenly become attentive at this description.*)

FALSTAFF. If I had it, I would have pawned it.

QUICKLY. Pretty fancy. Maltese, y'say?

WOOD. Do you know anything about Malta?

FALSTAFF. Malta is a Christian isle ruled by the Knights of Saint John. What saintly knights would want with a bejeweled dagger is beyond my understanding.

QUICKLY. How could you begin to understand a Christian knight? Virtue is beyond you.

FALSTAFF. As is temperance. Another round, Mistress.

WOOD. John, Nell, if you two could keep your ears peeled for anything about the knife, as well as about Archie, I'd appreciate it.

QUICKLY. It'll be a pleasure.

WOOD. And the other thing. This lady's kid brother. He's a guy named Sebastian. He's supposed to be in London, so if you see or hear about him…

QUICKLY. We shall contact you.

FALSTAFF. 'Twill be a pleasure to reunite the lad and sister. A mission of charity. And to properly dedicate us to our task, it is only right that our comrade Wood should treat us all to a round of sack to seal the bargain.

QUICKLY. The well's run dry for the night, Sir John.

FALSTAFF. Then I'm off to the Lupper's Head to seek rumor there. At the Lupper the drink flows 'til long after the night's final watch and who knows what tongues have been washed and flap upon the line? 'Til next we meet, my friend.

WOOD. Jack. I appreciate your help. If Archie were here, I'm sure...

FALSTAFF. Oh come now, murky Wood. Let us not distemper the night's revelry with such maudlin thoughts. Archie is well remembered and shall always be so in our hearts. And as for you Mistress Quickly, I shall return when thy wine stocks are not so miserly. 'Til morning then, my chuck. (*exits*)

QUICKLY (*sighing*) There are times when I am not certain whether it would be best for me to marry him or kill him. (*regards* **WOOD** *for a moment*) You all right, Wood?

WOOD. I'm fine. Just tired I guess.

QUICKLY. Well, here. (*places a bottle on the bar*) Courtesy of the house. Just don't let Sir John find out or he'll start thinkin' I'm givin' it away. Not that he pays for it anyway. (**WOOD** *pours himself a drink*) Aye, strange times we're in. Odd things abroad. There are those who drink here and say they have seen fairy light 'pon the square.

WOOD. Drinking this stuff I'm not surprised.

QUICKLY. Still your tongue. You've no need to drink it if you has complaints..

(**QUICKLY** *turns to leave, taking the bottle with her.*)

WOOD. Stop. Nell. I need a little companionship right now.

QUICKLY. Why, Woody. You flatter me.

WOOD. I was talking about the bottle.

(**QUICKLY** *angrily slams the bottle on the bar and exits. Left at the bar,* **WOOD** *looks at the bottle and then grabs a shot glass mysteriously left on the bar. He pours himself a drink. As he does, a second thug enters the bar and joins the first. This one is large and mean and radiates murderous intent. He is* **CATESBY**. *He gestures to* **WOOD** *and* **RATCLIFFE** *nods his understanding.* **WOOD** *doesn't see the thugs approaching, but he hears them draw their swords. He stiffens, but does not turn.*)

CATESBY. 'Tis a vile thing to die, my gracious lord, when men are unprepared and look not for it. *— make sure you don't block Rat-cliffe*

WOOD. I'm always prepared, but I never look for it.

RATCLIFFE. Turn and take thy blow to the forward face that men should not eulogize thee as a coward.

WOOD. A gentleman wouldn't stab a guy in the back.

RATCLIFFE. A gentleman hires me to do the deed. If thou shall not turn, then shall your back be pierced.

(*During this exchange the Stranger has stood up from his table and drawn his sword. He stands behind the thugs. He is a very handsome young man with a coiled spring energy barely kept in check. He views the world through wryly amused eyes and his name is* **MERCUTIO**.)

MERCUTIO. Thou hast pierced mine ears through, gentlemen. I would'st return the favor. If thou would'st do battle then cross steel with one who'st prepared and willing to cross thy purposes.

CATESBY. This is no quarrel of yours.

MERCUTIO. Aye, 'Tis true good sir. I have no quarrel with thee, Only thy blade. Stand away from the man.

(**CATESBY** *and* **RATCLIFFE** *part as if to leave, but then swing into action against* **MERCUTIO**. *The battle is furious, but even though outnumbered* **MERCUTIO** *not only manages to hold his own but overwhelms his opponents. After disarming one, he quickly picks up the blade. The remaining foe, now facing two blades, panics and rushes* *out with his partner.*)

MERCUTIO (*calling after them*) Run villains! Lest thy shadows
catch up with thee! (*laughing he joins* **WOOD** *at the bar,
there is a moment's silence*) What? No word of gratitude,
sir? I have saved thee from injury and death mayhap.
Have I rescued an ingrate?

WOOD. Thanks. (*he removes his hand from the pocket in which
he was holding his gun and places the weapon on the bar*)
I can take care of myself. (*pours another drink*) Why've
you been following me?

MERCUTIO (*laughs*) Thou saw'st. Thou art a singular man,
Mr. Wood. Shall we a duo be? Again, I have need to
speak to thee. My name is Mercutio, friend to the
house of Montague in fair Verona.

WOOD. Another Italian.

MERCUTIO. We are many scattered across the Boot, but as I
am the soul of virtue let me comfort thee that I mean
thee no harm. For the moment.

WOOD. What do you want?

MERCUTIO. I have come to these northern climes in search
of an artifact of the Montague clan. A bejeweled bodkin,
of which I believe you have some acquaintance.

WOOD. Never seen it, kid.

MERCUTIO. (*pause*) Thou need'st not be so knotty, Wood.
Such an ingratitude to offer one who has saved thy
life.

WOOD. For all I know you might've set all that up. I noticed
you let them get away unharmed.

MERCUTIO (*suddenly cold*) I am willing to slay if needs be.

WOOD. And just what would be those needs?

MERCUTIO. I would'st slay any who stands between myself
and the bodkin's return, be he peasant, rogue or private investigator.

WOOD. Someone like Archie Heath?

MERCUTIO. Art thou accusing me?

WOOD. Just asking.

MERCUTIO (*suddenly smiling*) Then ask you may. I knew not Archie Heath and I had no hand in his end, suspicious posture though it may be.

WOOD. Right.

MERCUTIO. Thou doubtest still my sincerity? Let me discourse upon my virtues so as thou might'st greater appreciate the delicate honor of my company.

WOOD. Don't put yourself out, Murray.

MERCUTIO. Mercutio!

WOOD. What ever.

MERCUTIO. I have killed before and should do so again if I had the cause. Remember that as I ask again. Where. Is. The. Knife?

WOOD. I don't know what you're talking about.

MERCUTIO. The dagger is the Montagues' right and my sworn obligation in aid of my friends in that house.

WOOD. I'll keep an eye for it.

MERCUTIO. We are prepared to make thee a wealthy man.

WOOD. I'll keep that in mind.

MERCUTIO. I am staying at the Centaur. Thou need'st but speak my name to the proprietress and I shall be found. (*starts to leave*)

WOOD. If I want to talk, I'll find you.

MERCUTIO. Thy life is owed to me, Mr. Wood.

WOOD. I owe you nothing.

(MERCUTIO *exits.* QUICKLY *re-enters looking after him.*)

QUICKLY. Who was that?

WOOD. Some guy. Looking for the knife.

QUICKLY. What's he want it for?

WOOD. Beats me. But unless I miss my guess, he'll be hanging around.

QUICKLY. So what are you going to do?

WOOD. I'm going to spend the night thinking. Leave the bottle. Bring another. I've got a lot of thinking to do.

QUICKLY. As you say.

(**QUICKLY** *slowly exits, leaving* **WOOD** *as he pours himself another drink. He raises it upwards as a toast.*)

WOOD. Another day and another day and another day, creepin' in from day to day until there ain't no more. And there ain't no more days for you, Archie. If a guy's life is just some time on stage then your show is over. Out, out, Heath cancelled. But I promise you, Archie. I'm gonna get the guy that done it. There's more to this case than just a bunch of sound and flurry. It's all gotta signify… somethin'.

(**WOOD** *downs the toast and then settles down into some serious boozing.*)

(*FADE OUT*)

- make sure to always cheat out.

10/23 —
We'll go more
over on Wednesday

Scene Three

(*The lights come up on the Boar's Head Tavern. It is dark and deserted save for the inert form of* **WOOD** *passed out on the bar. A number of empty bottles surround him. Somewhere a clock tolls the midnight hour.*

As **WOOD** *remains unconscious, a form moves in the dark. A small, nimble elf-like man detaches himself from the shadows. He rather amusedly surveys the scene. He is dressed in an odd costume recalling something of the forests and woodland glades. He approaches* **WOOD** *and then floats weightlessly onto the bar. He peers closely at* **WOOD** *and then examines one of the bottles. He "tsks" in mock admonition.* **PUCK** *brings his gaze within inches of* **WOOD**'*s face. Suddenly* **WOOD**'*s eyes snap open and he is looking directly into the little stranger's eyes.* **WOOD** *screams and falls off his bar stool.* **PUCK** *remains on the bar, laughing.*)

PUCK (*laughing*) Your kind never ceases to amuse me.

WOOD (*picking himself off the floor*) Who are you?

PUCK. You'll find it easier to get through this interview if you let me do the talking. Chances are you won't believe it anyway come morning.

WOOD. What time is it?

PUCK. 'Tis midnight. The hour when earth and heaven are at their closest. As to what I want, I have a message for you.

WOOD. Is this about the knife?

PUCK. In a manner, yes.

WOOD. Who are you?

PUCK. I am but a wanderer of the night and jester to the elven king. I am he who mocks the sons of Adam and frights the daughters of Eve. In short I am that merry spirit known as Robin Goodfellow of the Fair Folk, who is also called Puck.

WOOD. You're a fairy?

PUCK. A loaded word where you come from, but yes I am of the original variety.

WOOD. I get it. I'm drunk.

PUCK. Yes, you're pixilated. But I will not be dismissed as a mere illusion, mortal. I have too much pride for that. I have a warning for you, Mr. Wood.

WOOD. Not to mix bourbon and port?

PUCK. Please. You are mixed up in matters beyond your control.

WOOD. Tell me about it.

PUCK. Oh, I shall. Although you don't know it, you have been swept into the realms of divination and curses. On your present course you may soon be required to attempt to confound a prophecy. We who make our livelihood through such means must ensure the ultimate truthfulness of future sight.

WOOD. In other words, you want to see this prophecy come true.

PUCK. You have a way of cutting right to the heart of the matter, Mr. Wood.

WOOD. I don't know anything about any prophecy. And I don't want to know. But as hallucinations go this one is pretty tame, so let's stretch this out before the elephants arrive. What's the prophecy?

PUCK. A number of years ago some women of our number predicted a certain person would become king.

(*silence*)

WOOD. And?

PUCK. And that's it. A certain person will become king.

WOOD. No names? No places?

PUCK. It's prediction not prescription.

WOOD. And this is the prophecy that I'm going to screw up somehow?

PUCK. Colorfully, but succinctly put.

WOOD. King of what? King of England? King of France? King of the Hill?

- watch to make sure

PUCK. That's prophecy for you. Deep in meaning, short on detail.

WOOD. I don't care about any friggin' fortune tellin.'

PUCK. Shall we test it? Come here. You may ask me three questions, but they must each be different.

WOOD. Why?

PUCK. Because it amuses me. Ask.

WOOD. Who killed Archie? ~~Skip around~~

PUCK. A mortal. (*he laughs himself off the bar and has to pull himself back up*) Ask another question.

WOOD. That's no answer. Who killed Archie?

PUCK. You already asked that question, bucko. Pay attention to the rules.

WOOD. Damn you.

PUCK. Already done.

WOOD. Why was he killed?

PUCK. Because he was thought to have a certain something.

WOOD. What? What did he have?

PUCK. Is that your question?

(**WOOD** *grabs* **PUCK** *by the shirtfront*) _Keep in mind Hannah

WOOD. I'm tired of being jerked around. In one night I've been threatened, attacked and warned, and I still don't know what's going on. I've got a knife everyone wants, but will anyone tell me why? No! I'm caught in a crossfire and I don't even know who the targets are. And now I've got some friggin' elf who won't give me a straight answer.

PUCK. I'm not answering. I'm prophesying. (*pulls himself free and straightens his shirt with wounded dignity*) I'm trying to help you, buckaroo. Watch your back and watch your step. You've got people after you and you've got people who want to see you dead.

WOOD. Because of the case?

PUCK. Yup.

WOOD. Why, damn it?

PUCK. If you swear you'll catch no fish.

WOOD. That's no answer. That's a fortune cookie.

PUCK. Consider it sort of a warning.

WOOD. I ain't afraid.

PUCK. But then you don't know it all yet. Watch yourself. Things aren't always what they seem.

WOOD. I guess you'd know all about that.

PUCK. That I do. Happy trails, pardner. (*floats away*)

WOOD. God. This better all be a dream.

(*BLACK OUT*)

Day 2 — no change of clothes for wood, he's drunk. 2 Tis hanging on coat rack.

Scene Four

WOOD (*addresses the audience*) I woke up the next morning with my face pressed into the hard reality of Nell's bar. I'd been there before. I barely had time to get back to the office to meet the guy I told Charlotte to get. Donalbain was royalty. He'd been spending his time sponging off the courts of Europe using the excuse of exile to get free room and board. He never had a scrap of pride. But he knew all the right people. And he was willing to help.

(**WOOD** *enters the scene. It is morning in his office and* **WOOD** *is pouring himself another drink while nursing a monster of a hangover. In the client's chair is* **DONALBAIN**, *dispossessed prince of Scotland. An unambitious young noble fond of slumming and always in need of a buck. He is impeccably dressed and lounges in the attitude of one thoroughly satisfied with his place in the world.*)

DONALBAIN. Art thou well, old sport? Thou seemest to be ill.

WOOD. Just a flu bug. Nothing for you to worry about. So what do you know about the knife?

DONALBAIN. Never heard of such a thing to tell the truth. A Maltese cross you say? And Italians?

WOOD. Yeah. They're crawling out of the woodwork.

DONALBAIN. 'Tis a puzzlement, I'm afraid. Did you ask the King?

WOOD. His highness only deals with me on the QT. I don't ask any favors of him and he don't ask any favors of me. (*struck by a thought*) Donny. You're a prince, right?

DONALBAIN. I suffer from that hereditary illness, yes.

WOOD. Ever want to be king?

DONALBAIN. Good God no.

WOOD. No one ever, um, predicted you'd be king did they?

DONALBAIN. Hardly. My brother Malcolm was the older. He was always to be king. 'Twas my station to be chancellor or prime minister or some other such foolish thing. Instead I fled the country in fear of my life and now spend my declining years as a guest of various European courts. Smartest thing I've ever done.

WOOD. Listen. You know what I want you to do?

DONALBAIN. I will certainly be happy to enquire about the court on your behalf. Discreetly of course. If the knife was seen by anyone at the London court I will soon find out. Might I be able to see the weapon in question? I know a fair amount about daggers. A professional interest, you understand.

(**WOOD** *removes the bodkin from his desk drawer and hands it to* **DONALBAIN**)

WOOD. A lot of people seem to be interested in that hardware.

DONALBAIN. And well they should. It's a magnificent piece. Though only a connoisseur would pick up the real details. The jewels for instance are rather cheap, almost glass really. But it is exquisitely made. I see the cross, but I would say this is Italian made really. Not a weapon of war, but something to wear in court. A knight wouldn't be caught dead wearing it, but it would thrill any blue blood I know. And this was found in poor Archie's back? That's a crime.

WOOD. Yeah. Murder.

DONALBAIN. What I meant was that it's a waste of material. Any old kitchen carver could kill a man, but why waste such a magnificent tool on a peasant? Especially Archie.

WOOD. I'm sorry we don't meet your exacting standards, Donny.

DONALBAIN. I'm sorry, Wood. Nothing personal. I liked Archie. And I shall be more than happy to help you solve this mystery.

WOOD. Thanks.

DONALBAIN. And if you have any other task you wish to set me, please feel free to ask.

WOOD. Thanks, Don. But...

DONALBAIN. You have lost a partner and I have lost a friend. Aye, Archie was both these things. And now you are short of help. Fortunately I am willing to offer assistance.

WOOD. Just getting information on the knife will be enough.

DONALBAIN. And what will you be doing?

WOOD. Tracking down this lady's brother. This Sebastian.

DONALBAIN. Indeed. Then perhaps I could-

(*There is a knock on the door.* **CHARLOTTE** *sticks her head in.*)

CHARLOTTE. Sorry to interrupt, but Miss da Messaline is here to see you.

WOOD. Gimme a sec. (*straightens up the room and himself as* **CHARLOTTE** *ducks back into the outer office*)

DONALBAIN. And this is your client, hm? I'm quite anxious to meet her.

WOOD (*struggling into his jacket and straightening his tie*) All right. You can stay. Just keep quiet and stay out of the way.

DONALBAIN. You won't even know I'm here.

(**WOOD** *sees* **DONALBAIN** *is still holding the bodkin. He motions for its return. Just as* **WOOD** *receives the knife, the door opens and* **CHARLOTTE** *shows* **VIOLA** *into the room.* **VIOLA** *pauses in the doorway and watches* **WOOD** *return the knife to his desk drawer.* **CHARLOTTE** *returns to her station.*)

WOOD. (*noticing* **VIOLA** *staring at* **DONALBAIN**) Don't worry about Don. He's a friend who knows how to keep his mouth shut.

DONALBAIN. I am providing assistance on your case.

VIOLA. Indeed.

WOOD. So what brings you down to my office this early in the morning?

VIOLA. As I was through my chattels searching, an image of my brother was discoveréd. I bring it to thy hunter's aid until Sebastian is recoveréd.

WOOD. A picture should make things easier.

DONALBAIN. I should like to see it also. So that I might assist thee.

WOOD. So? Where is it?

VIOLA. Thou must see it now?

WOOD. It couldn't hurt.

VIOLA. Perhaps 'Tis so.

DONALBAIN. There's no reason to be afraid.

WOOD. We're all friends here.

DONALBAIN. Aye.

VIOLA. I say, most gentle sir. Thy name is Don?

DONALBAIN. 'Tis what Wood calls me. My name is Donalbain.

WOOD. But don't hold that against him.

VIOLA. Most comely name,

DONALBAIN. Thou wouldst flatter me.

VIOLA. Nay, sir. I assure thee not.

WOOD. If we could get back to business –

VIOLA (*suddenly*) I was followed.

WOOD. What?

VIOLA. From the Dolphin to thy door.

WOOD. Why didn't you mention this earlier?

VIOLA. He is a roguish man of furtive glance and mien. And by his side I stole a glance of his rapier's vicious gleam.

(**WOOD** *peers out the window, his weapon drawn.* **DONALBAIN** *is soon by his side.*)

DONALBAIN. Dost thou spy the man?

WOOD. Yeah, I think I've got him spotted.

DONALBAIN. Who is he?

WOOD. A cheap little thug named Iago. He's movin! (*rushes to the door*)

DONALBAIN. Allow me, Wood. I can keep an eye on Iago.

WOOD. Donny, this could be dangerous.

DONALBAIN. I grew up around dangerous, Wood. Surely if I could survive a court full of intriguers and plotters, I could handle a paltry criminal. And besides, you must begin your search for the fine lady's brother.

WOOD. Donny…

VIOLA. Our friend Donalbain speaks most wisely, Wood. Decide most quickly else Iago flee for good.

WOOD (*considers, then turns to* **DONALBAIN**) Just follow. Don't take any chances.

DONALBAIN. Ah, but this is excitement. You shall not regret this, Wood.

(**DONALBAIN** *exits.* **VIOLA** *holds a cameo out to* **WOOD**.)

WOOD. What's that?

VIOLA. My brother's image. Pressed to thy service. Guard it well.

WOOD (*examining the portrait*) So… This is your brother. Young.

VIOLA. Young when the image was crafted.

WOOD. You don't have a more recent one?

VIOLA. Nay. Our family has not many portraits. We like them not.

WOOD. I've got people looking in Eastcheap. Today I'll talk to some merchants.

VIOLA. 'Tis wise.

WOOD. It's the only way to start.

VIOLA. Shall I accompany thee?

WOOD. No. I want you out of this. I've already got one murder on my hands, I don't want to risk your pretty little neck.

VIOLA. Thou art too kind.

WOOD. Merely cautious.

VIOLA. I meant about the neck.

WOOD. I want you to go back to your hotel room. I'll call you if I need any more information. (*opens the door for her*)

VIOLA. As you wish. (*crosses to* **WOOD**) I am so glad thou hast agreed to work on my behalf.

(**VIOLA** *exits.* **WOOD** *stands still holding the door. He whistles in admiration.* **CHARLOTTE** *enters.*)

CHARLOTTE. Yeah. She's a hot one all right.

WOOD. Charlotte. I got a job for you, hon.

CHARLOTTE. A job? Whataya want me to do?

WOOD. Do you know anyone smart?

CHARLOTTE. Um…

WOOD. I need some information on the Knights of Malta.

CHARLOTTE. Sure. I'll go find a historian or somethin'.

WOOD. Good.

CHARLOTTE. Anything for you, boss.

WOOD. Right. (*grabbing his hat and coat*) So get your tail movin'. We got a busy day ahead of us.

(**WOOD** *and* **CHARLOTTE** *exit through the office door.*)

(*FADE OUT*)

Scene Five

WOOD (*addressing audience*) The first thing any shamus learns is that ninety five percent of the job is following down leads that lead to nothing. And that's what I got lookin' for Sebastian. One big zero after another. Maybe he was hiding. Maybe he didn't want to be found. Maybe he was afraid) Maybe he was shy.

The second thing a shamus learns is that whenever you can't find the guy you're looking for, you'll always find the last guy you want to meet. This time it was in the market at Saint Paul's...

(WOOD turns to exit but he is stopped a shout.)

FANG. (entering) 'Ere, Wood! I've been looking for you.

(The scene shifts to the sights and sounds the St. Paul's market. A bustling locale located in the yards of the cathedral. Almost every kind of good both old and new is for sale here. It is the kind of place bound to attract criminals and so it is not surprising to find officers of the law here, even ones like SERGEANT FANG.

FANG is a slovenly brute. Although a lawman he is really only a single step up from the criminals he apprehends. He is the kind of cop more concerned about his private retirement fund than the law, even though he consistently uses his badge as a bludgeon and a lever.

Knowing there is no escape, WOOD turns to meet FANG.)

WOOD. Sergeant Fang. What brings you to this neck of the woods? They get tired of you stinking up the waterfront?

FANG. I'll remind you that I'm an officer of the law.

WOOD. Ever wonder why people keep forgetting that, Fang?

FANG. Listen 'ere, Wood. The word on the street is that you're lookin' into Archie Heath's murder.

WOOD. He was my partner.

don't all enter from the same side

FANG. It's a police matter. *My* police matter.

WOOD. You're the investigating officer on the case?

FANG. I don't appreciate people opening books on cases, especially when I closed them personally myself. It was an open and shut case.

WOOD. A little too quickly open and shut.

FANG. Heath was attacked by a single knife wound to the back. Probably attacked by some low grade cutpurse. It happens all the time.

WOOD. With officers like you around, I ain't surprised. Listen, I think I got a new angle on this case. Aren't you even interested?

FANG. I'm only interested in keeping things quiet. You're sticking your nose in where it don't belong. And if you're not careful, I'll clip it off for you. Understood?

WOOD. Yeah, I can decode your metaphor, Fang. But I'll tell you this. Archie was my partner. That may not mean a lot to you, but it means an awful lot to me. And if you think I'm going to sit still while his killer is still walking the street, then you have another think coming.

FANG. You talk big, Wood. But I'm telling you, If there was any way to catch this bloke I would have found it.

WOOD. You couldn't find your way out of a closet.

FANG. You watch out, Wood. You're going to need me some-day. And on that day you'll knock on my door and I'll laugh in your face. Count on it. (*whirls and exits*)

WOOD (*to himself*) Lord. What other idiots are walking loose?

MERCUTIO (*entering*) Mr. Wood! Well met!

WOOD. Damn. (*turns to face* **MERCUTIO**) It's you again. Murray.

MERCUTIO. Mercutio.

WOOD. What ever.

MERCUTIO. Hast thou found the dagger yet?

WOOD. I ain't looking for a knife. I'm looking for a kid. Maybe you seen him?

(**WOOD** *passes* **MERCUTIO** *the portrait. He examines it closely.*)

MERCUTIO. Apologies, friend Wood. I have ne'er before beheld the boy. (*passes back the portrait*) What is his connection to the Maltese Bodkin?

WOOD. What makes you think there's a connection?

MERCUTIO. What makest thou think so?

WOOD. I don't. The kid's a welcher. Owes me money.

MERCUTIO (*not taken in*) As thou sayest. (*pause*) It strikes me, Wood, that thou art like the dead man buried with his skull pointing down. Thou art in over thy head. Those men who attacked thee last night, they were not any ordinary thugs. They work for the Duke.

WOOD. The Duke? What does he want?

MERCUTIO. The bodkin, I suspect. Art thou ready to oppose one such as the Duke when thou knowest not even the nature of the game?

WOOD. And you do?

MERCUTIO. I am apprising thee of the players am I not?

WOOD. And what makes you so eager to help?

MERCUTIO. I want the knife, my friend. And I believest thou can fetch it for me. And 'til thou canst, I shall try to keep the hounds off thy back. Though I cannot help thee if thou art determined to brave the wolf pack by thyself.

WOOD. Thanks for the warning. (*starts to leave*)

MERCUTIO. And if I were thee, I would keep a careful watch on the bitch.

WOOD (*stops and turns*) The bitch?

MERCUTIO. Or is that stretching the canine metaphor too far? Beware the lady, my friend.

WOOD. What makes you think I should be afraid of Miss da Messaline? What do you know about her? Why should I even listen?

MERCUTIO. As to thy last question first, I fear thou art in dire danger. As to thy second question next, I only know what I saw and only ten nights past I saw her remove a knife from a man's back. Which answers thy first question last. She is cold and calculating. Even in the face of death. Most unwomanly say I, and so cool as to be inhuman say I.

WOOD. I make my own judgments when it comes to women, Murray.

MERCUTIO. Mercutio!

WOOD. Whatever. (*exits*)

MERCUTIO (*calling after him*) Then 'Tis thine own funeral, dear Wood. And the hand that rocks thee to that final sleep shall not be mine. Farewell.

(**MERCUTIO** *exits*)

(*FADE OUT*)

Scene Six

WOOD (*addressing the audience*) I don't trust guardian angels. But all that talk about the knife got me thinking. And the more I thought about it, the more I thought that that thing had to be put some place safer than my desk drawer. But before I left the Market I found something that I thought could help. Buying the book, that was a hunch. Hiding the knife, that was a necessity.

(*The office. Night. There is a figure seated in the dark behind* **WOOD***'s desk.* **WOOD** *enters through the office door. He has a book under one arm. As he enters he sees the note taped to the door's glass panel.*)

WOOD (*reading the note*) "Dear Bernie, I found a book on those Knights. It's on your desk. See you in the morning. Charlotte."

(*Smiling,* **WOOD** *reaches to switch on the lights. There is the soft click of the switch, but nothing happens. He tries again with the same result. Now certain that something is wrong,* **WOOD** *draws his gun and cautiously enters the room. Moving carefully he scouts the room until he spots the person seated in his chair.*)

WOOD. All right. Whoever you are. I gotcha covered.

DONALBAIN. Wood?

WOOD (*holstering his weapon*) Donny. What are you doing here?

(**DONALBAIN** *shakily gets out of the chair and unsteadily stands frame in the window.*)

DONALBAIN. Wood, I... (*suddenly topples forward*)

WOOD. Donny! (**WOOD** *rushes forward and catches* **DONALBAIN** *in his arms.*)

DONALBAIN. Wood. Iago. He works... The Duke...

(*With a final gasp* **DONALBAIN** *rolls fatally forward in* **WOOD***'s arms revealing the Maltese Bodkin sticking out of his back.*)

(*FADE OUT*)

END OF ACT ONE

Day 3

ACT TWO

Scene One

(*We find* **WOOD** *standing in an isolating light. He regards the hat in his hand in a contemplative pose. He slowly turns his attention to the audience as the saxophone wails.*)

WOOD. Alas, poor Donalbain. I knew him. (*slowly places the hat back on his head*) Well... I was no closer to solving this case and here was another friend dead. I wasn't there for Archie. And I hadn't been there for Donny. If I didn't do something quick, I wasn't going to have any pals left.

(*The office, the next morning.* **WOOD** *is sitting at his desk as he reads from the book he purchased at the Market.*)

WOOD. "But when I came unto my beds,
　　With a hey, ho, the wind and the rain,
　　With tosspots still had drunken heads,
　　For the rain it raineth every day."
　　"A great while ago the world begun,
　　With hey, ho, the wind and the rain,
　　But that's all one, our play is done,
　　And we'll strive to please you every day."

(**WOOD** *pauses to take a drink. There is the sound of someone singing "The Lady is a Tramp" in the outer office. The door opens and* **CHARLOTTE** *enters. She jumps when she sees* **WOOD**.)

CHARLOTTE. Geez. You gave me a heart attack. Whatcha doin' here so early?

WOOD. I didn't go home.

CHARLOTTE. Didn't you get my note?

WOOD. I saw the note.

CHARLOTTE. So you weren't waitin'. So what were you doing? Reading? Boy, that's two things I never thought I'd see you doin'. One's you sitting here first thing in the morning and the other is seeing you read. Not that I ever thought you couldn't, but you gotta admit-

WOOD. Charlotte! (*beat*) Donalbain's dead.

CHARLOTTE. Oh, geez. When...?

WOOD (*reaching for his bottle*) Last night. Here in the office. The knife was in his back. (*pours himself a drink*)

CHARLOTTE. Which knife? Oh. *The* knife. (*beat*) So. Wahtcha going to do about it?

(**WOOD** *pauses, the drink inches away from his mouth.*)

WOOD. What?

CHARLOTTE. Whatcha going to do? I mean, you're the boss right? We got a case. We *are* going to do something. Or are we gonna keep on doing things the way we've been doin'?

(**WOOD** *pauses and then looks at the drink in his hand.*)

WOOD. (*making a firm decision*) No. (*he puts the glass down*) We're not going to keep on doing things the same way we've been doing. I'm sick of everybody knowing what's going on except for me. We're going to start changing things. But first you gotta do something for me, doll.

CHARLOTTE. Anything.

WOOD. (*opens the desk drawer and removes the knife*) I want you to hide this for me.

CHARLOTTE. Hey, that's the –

WOOD. The little killer herself. I took it out of Donny. The cops don't know about it. Take it.

CHARLOTTE. I don't...

WOOD. Take it. It won't bite. I even cleaned it. Cleaned it... (*a thought occurs to him and he examines the knife more closely*) I wiped it with a cloth. Still a little blood in the detail work. A knick where the blade hit one of Donny's vertebrae. (*noticing the queasy* **CHARLOTTE**) Charlotte. Hide this thing. Don't tell anyone where it is. Not even me. If anything happens to me, I want you to wait a couple days and then take the knife to the law.

CHARLOTTE. You mean Fang?

WOOD. He's the officer in charge of the case. Just make sure he doesn't lose it like the knives in the Caesar case.

CHARLOTTE. Got it.

WOOD. (*grabbing his hat and heading for the door*) Good. Don't come back to the office until noon. Word won't be really circulating on the street until then anyway.

CHARLOTTE. Word? What word?

WOOD. The word I'm going to start spreading around.

(**WOOD** *exits.* **CHARLOTTE** *walks over to* **WOOD**'s *desk and picks up the book he was reading. She reads the title printed on the spine.*)

CHARLOTTE. The... Complete Works... of... William Shakespeare?

(**CHARLOTTE** *is confused and we leave her that way as the scene blacks out.*)

(*BLACK OUT*)

Scene Two

(The Boar's Head Tavern, morning. Chairs have been placed upside down on tables. **FALSTAFF** *can be seen sleeping with his head on the bar. He snores loudly.* **WOOD** *enters and spots* **FALSTAFF***.)*

WOOD. Sir John? Jack?

(There is no response. **WOOD** *finds a half filled bottle on the bar. After a moment's consideration, he pours the contents on* **FALSTAFF***'s head. He awakes with a start.)*

FALSTAFF. 'Twas not I! I was in the vespers all night! *(getting his bearings, he focuses on* **WOOD***)* Oh. 'Tis you. Have you no respect for a man who hath labored on thy behalf? If not the man, then respect the sack. Pour it not upon mine locks but down my throat if needs be. Such waste ill becomes thee, Wood.

WOOD. Have you found the kid yet?

FALSTAFF. Kid? Oh yes, the lad. His name escapes me for the…

WOOD. Sebastian.

FALSTAFF. As I was about to say. This very day shall my subordinates resume thy cause, although not this very hour. When the sun lies in slumber in the sky, then who am I, modest knight that I am, to dispute such celestial example? As a humble knight I shall not rise 'til Apollo too is riz.

WOOD. In other words, you don't started until noon.

FALSTAFF. Thou fail'st to grasp my philosophy, but thou hast found the truth of it. Wood, if thou wouldst allow an old knight to speak his mind… I think this lad is not within my territories. The boy who you described to me could scarce be living in Eastcheap's gentle courtesies without being remarked upon. A youngling of noble mien and character? If he be not lying in a ditch he would be a source of merriment to every scamp and fishwife.

WOOD. It's a long shot I admit, but I'd like you to keep looking. And if you could do something else for me...

FALSTAFF. My head tympanates.

WOOD. A small job.

FALSTAFF. How small?

WOOD. Very small.

FALSTAFF. A thing so small could be lost behind the seat cushions. Leave it there to find in the afternoon.

(**QUICKLY** *enters straightening up*)

QUICKLY. Woody! Well met. 'Tis an early hour for ye, i'nt it? Here, has Sir John been giving you trouble?

FALSTAFF. No trouble. I am too drowsy to create conflict.

WOOD. I need your help.

QUICKLY. Not more boarders? Those two cravens are two enough to cook for.

WOOD. How are Tweedle Dee and Tweedle Dum?

QUICKLY. Still feared they are to be executed. They are unconvinced of the counterfeit's detection.

WOOD. A forgery is easy to spot if you spell the king's name wrong three times.

QUICKLY. Still. They hide in shadows.

WOOD. I'll check on them later. Listen, you two. I need a message spread around town.

FALSTAFF. Tut. (*pats stomach*) I have spread enough already. (*laughs*)

QUICKLY. Still yourself. What's the message?

WOOD. The Maltese Bodkin will found in the cemetery of St. Mark's, midnight tonight.

QUICKLY. What's your plan, Woody?

WOOD. I'm throwing out some bait, Nell. I got to see who snaps it up.

QUICKLY. Make certain well 'tis not yourself who gets snapped up.

WOOD. Will you do it?

QUICKLY. If you're certain, aye. 'Twill be on every lip in

Eastcheap before the supper hour.

FALSTAFF. And I shall report thy missive in every hostel *after* the supper hour. But if I am to do thy service, I shall require my fullest strength. And so I to bed. Good day to you, my friend. And good morrow to you my faithful Mistress Nell. (*he sinks behind the bar*)

QUICKLY. You're sure about this are ye?

WOOD. I'm not sure about anything. But I need to get a handle on this case. If everyone who wants that friggin' knife shows up I may get something I can use.

QUICKLY. A four foot hole. Or worse. I hope you know what you're doing.

WOOD. I know what I'm doing. I'm meeting the problem head on. (*exits*)

QUICKLY (*calling after him*) Like a bull. Into a brick wall!

(*FADE OUT*)

Scene Three

(*The cemetery of St. Mark's. It is very nearly midnight.
A number of ancient gravestones surround the area and
a heavy mist floats over the ground. A form moves in
the moonlight and resolves itself into a wary* **IAGO**. *He
searches the yard and finds no one. There is the call of
an owl and* **IAGO** *is so startled he draws his sword.
He quickly calms himself, but keeps his weapon at the
ready.*)

MERCUTIO (*offstage*) Ill met by moonlight.

(**IAGO** *quickly turns to confront the voice.* **MERCUTIO**
casually enters.)

MERCUTIO. It is said that to safely uncover the root of
the mandragula one must pluck it from the earth of
a churchyard at midnight. But lest the scream of the
magic root drive you mad when evicted from its home,
one must first stop up one's ears with wax and smother
all sounds with trumps and bells. A complex operation
to be sure, but the root is known to be the source of
the one true love tincture. Mind you, I place my faith
In those gifts that nature hath endowed me with and
so I have never found the need-

[handwritten in margin: slow this down]

IAGO. Are you the one?

MERCUTIO. I am one and always one. A state to which I am
accustomed. Who dost thou seek?

IAGO. Have you it? Give it to me.

MERCUTIO. As I am a charitable soul, I shall endeavor to
satisfy thy pleas, though please it may myself. What
is it thou seek'st? Salvation on a moon bedewed
churchyard? Or the piety of thy grave ancestors? Or-

IAGO. Have you the bodkin?

MERCUTIO. Nay, sir.

IAGO. Then why are you here?

MERCUTIO. I claim the knife by rights of oath and honor.

IAGO. You are a thief.

MERCUTIO. I speak of rights and thou wrongest me.

IAGO. The Bodkin you want?

MERCUTIO. Yes. And you?

IAGO. Will have it.

MERCUTIO. 'Tis not thine.

IAGO. It shall be.

MERCUTIO. Thou hast no claim.

IAGO. You will fight for it?

MERCUTIO. I will kill for it. Begone, scraphound.

IAGO. You scare not I.

MERCUTIO. More fool thee. I have an obligation to fulfill. Honor may only be regained through its recovery.

IAGO. The blade you claim is another's.

(**MERCUTIO** *has turned his back to* **IAGO** *who attacks with his sword.* **MERCUTIO** *evades the assault and draws his sword.* **MERCUTIO** *returns the attack with skills honed on the combative streets of Verona.* **IAGO** *and* **MERCUTIO** *battle amongst the gravestones. Both are talented duelists and neither gains the upper hand for very long. Echoing the ringing blades, the chimes of midnight are heard. Finally* **IAGO** *is forced over a stone and he tumbles backwards, although he retains his sword in hand.* **MERCUTIO** *stands over him.*)

MERCUTIO. Get thee hence. I give thee thy life's liberty. Depart and –

(**IAGO** *throws a handful of dirt into* **MERCUTIO** *'s eyes. Blinded,* **MERCUTIO** *cannot defend himself from* **IAGO** *'s vicious kick to the solar plexus.* **MERCUTIO** *lies in pain as* **IAGO** *raises his sword to deliver the killing blow.*)

WOOD (*entering with pistol drawn*) All right. Hold it right there. (**IAGO** *freezes*) Back off, pal. Before I drill you. (**IAGO** *pauses, then quickly runs off*)

MERCUTIO (*getting up*) My thanks. If thou hadst not come when thou didst…

WOOD. I was coming any way.

MERCUTIO. Thou art the source of the message?

WOOD. Yep.

MERCUTIO. Then thou hast found the bodkin?

WOOD. Nope.

MERCUTIO. I see.

WOOD. What's so important about that piece?

MERCUTIO. 'Tis a Montague family heirloom.

WOOD. Don't play dumb. There's more to this thing than a bunch of guys arguing about antiques.

MERCUTIO. By what right should I answer thee?

WOOD. I just saved your life.

MERCUTIO. As I saved thine.

WOOD. Yeah, but that don't mean a thing to a guy like me. I have a feeling your one of guys who can't let something like that go.

MERCUTIO. Thou art…

WOOD. Right.

MERCUTIO. Right. I owe thee a service. But the matter of the bodkin is one of sworn obligation. It o'erpowers any debt that I might owe to thee.

WOOD. I need some answers here, kid.

MERCUTIO. I cannot betray the Montagues' trust. In any other manner I would'st be glad to honor thy claim.

WOOD. Right now all I care about is my partner. (*pause*) You said you saw Miss da Messaline pull a knife out of a guy's back. Did she see you?

MERCUTIO. I think not. 'Twas dark. The only light spilled from the window above.

WOOD. What about the stiff?

MERCUTIO. I know not who the man was.

WOOD. He was my partner. Do you know who killed him?

MERCUTIO. I know not.

WOOD. Was it you?

MERCUTIO. Sirrah!

WOOD. Your own words put you at the scene of the crime, Murray.

MERCUTIO. I know not who killed thy friend. (*beat*) I understand. 'Tis a matter of honor for thee. We are much alike –

WOOD. Beat it.

MERCUTIO. There is a debt between us. It shall be resolved, I swear. (*exits*)

WOOD. I won't hold my breath. (*sits on a gravestone and ponders.*)

VOICE. Stubborn lad, is he not? (**WOOD** *starts and jumps to his feet with his pistol drawn*) But then the citizens of Verona have always been too intractable for their own good. The kind of people who would kill their own sons rather than kiss their enemies. I fear no good will come of it.

WOOD. Who's there?

VOICE. I come in response to the invitation that you issued.

WOOD. I prefer to see who I'm talking to.

VOICE. Very well.

(*A distinguished man in the elegant robes of a mystic scholar steps into the moonlight. He is in late middle age and projects an air of confidence and detached amusement. He is* **PROSPERO**.)

PROSPERO. Thou hast questions. Allow me to anticipate your first by means of introduction. I am the reigning Duke of Milan, Prospero by name.

WOOD. What is this? Everyone in Italy decide to come to England for the summer?

PROSPERO. I am not in England. I rest in my palace in Milan.

WOOD. Take a look around, genius. Your palace has a few more stiffs than local building codes allow.

PROSPERO. I have sent my spirit 'cross the waters to speak to thee.

WOOD. Gee. Thanks. And how do you do that? More dny

PROSPERO. Through sorcery and means arcane.

WOOD. You're a duke *and* a magician?

PROSPERO. In the Italian courts you require every advantage Fate allowest.

WOOD. No kidding.

PROSPERO. I am concerned about the knife.

WOOD. Isn't everyone? (*he turns to leave*)

PROSPERO. It could confound the prophecy. (**WOOD** *freezes*) Ah. That got your attention.

WOOD. What prophecy?

PROSPERO. What prophecy dost thou think?

WOOD. The only one I heard recently was about some guy becoming king.

PROSPERO. And what else?

WOOD. That's it.

PROSPERO (*sighing*) Fairy spirits can be a little too secretive for their own good. They have a horrible tendency to couch everything in riddles. Most annoying.

WOOD. You're telling me.

PROSPERO. And tell I shall, Mr. Wood. You must understand that we of the sorcerous fraternity have an interest in seeing that once a prediction is made, it comes true. And so if some witch says that some boy is going to become king, he must.

WOOD. So you're a union man. Which witch?

PROSPERO. Witch, witch, witch. Three witches actually. Up in Scotland. In the lower ranks of the Art really. But if they make a prediction for someone… ~~I~~ not actually

WOOD. Wait a minute. This someone. Just who might that be?

PROSPERO. The usurper king of Scotland. Among other things he was told that the descendants of his best friend would become kings.

WOOD. So, what did this schmuck do?

PROSPERO. He tried to have his best friend and his son killed. Messy business actually.

WOOD. Tried?

PROSPERO. Good. You pay attention to details. The father was indeed slain, but his son fled to England to eventually sire a line of English kings.

WOOD. And this is the prophecy you're afraid will be stopped?

PROSPERO. He must be allowed to sire the line of kings. It has been so prophesied.

WOOD. But how can the knife screw up your predictions? Is it magic or something?

PROSPERO. The dagger possess no mystic potential. The power it represents is temporal.

WOOD. What power?

PROSPERO. The power of the Knights of Malta. Thou must be cautious, Mr. Wood.

(*Unseen by* WOOD, IAGO *re-enters and advances on* WOOD*'s back. He has a cudgel.*)

WOOD. I got things under control.

PROSPERO. Things are not always what they seem. Remember that. I fear this interview is at an end.

WOOD. What's that supposed to mean?

PROSPERO. A pleasure meeting you, Mr. Wood.

WOOD. Now, wait. I –

(IAGO *brings the cudgel down on* WOOD*'s head. He falls unconscious.*)

PROSPERO. Now that must have hurt.

IAGO. Talking to yourself in a graveyard, Mr. Wood. Some losing your mind would think you are. (PROSPERO *fades away*) And now, Mr. Wood, we go to meet the Duke.

(IAGO *lifts the unconscious detective as the lights*

(*FADE OUT*)

Scene Four

(*A dismal light finds* **WOOD** *still unconscious and tied to a chair. The place could anywhere or nowhere. Nothing is seen but the darkness, the chair and* **WOOD**. **IAGO** *enters. He regards* **WOOD** *with gloating pleasure. He lightly slaps Wood on the cheek.*)

IAGO. Wake up, Mr. Wood. Wake up.

(**WOOD** *makes consciousness raising sounds. Three shadowy figures enter, but remain out of the light. The central figure makes a signal and the burliest figure steps into the light. It is* **CATESBY**. *He stands by* **WOOD** *and then looks back for a cue. One of the darkened figures, the leader, nods.* **CATESBY** *winds up and delivers a bruising slap to* **WOOD**'s *cheek. When* **WOOD** *lifts his head he is awake and in pain.*)

IAGO. Hello, Mr. Wood. Awake you are now? Good. You have things to tell.

CATESBY. Where is the Maltese Bodkin?

IAGO. Sir William Catesby is my friend here. A dangerous man he is. Impatient too. He does not care to wait for answers he does.

CATESBY. Where is the Maltese Bodkin?

IAGO. A charming conversationalist is he not? I fear if he asks again he shall expect an answer. (*beat*) No reply, Mr. Wood? An unfortunate circumstance this is. And over what will you be killed? A meaningless little weapon that you realize not even the importance of. A tragedy this is. But Sir William Catesby is, as I said, an impatient man.

CATESBY. Where is the Maltese Bodkin? Where is the Maltese Bodkin? Where is the Maltese Bodkin?

(**CATESBY** *begins to hit* **WOOD**. *The leader clears his throat.* **IAGO** *and* **CATESBY** *immediately give him their attention. The leader shakes his head and the two men back into the half-light leaving* **WOOD** *isolated.*

The leader limps into the light. He is an ugly, twisted figure with a shriveled hand and a hunchback. He is dressed all in black. His attitude is one of unshakable confidence and absolute control. This is, of course, **RICHARD**, *Duke of Gloucester. He pauses, examining* **WOOD** *from one angle and then moves to another. At all times* **WOOD** *watches* **RICHARD** *as closely as one would watch a poisonous snake. He is not far wrong.*)

RICHARD. So. This is the one man who has been giving us so much trouble?

IAGO. Yes, my grace. He –

RICHARD. (*raises his hand to silence* **IAGO**) Do you know who I am, Mr. Wood? I am Richard, Duke of Gloucester and, by the grace of God and whoever else, soon to be thy king. You are… You are looking at my hump are you not?

WOOD. No, I…

RICHARD. Go ahead and look. I don't mind. I not only admit my ugliness, I embrace it. It allows me to see the world for how ugly it really is. Do you want to see me limp? It's not a pretty sight.

WOOD. That's okay. I don't –

RICHARD. No, no. Please indulge me. Watch me walk. (*he demonstrates his limp*) Pathetic, isn't it?

WOOD. Well, I don't know…

RICHARD. If I say something's pathetic then it is pathetic. I know pathetic and this walk is pathetic.

IAGO. Oh yes, my lord. Wonderfully pathetic. — Richard-stop Iago away

RICHARD. I know everything that's wrong with the world because it is reflected in me. It is that which will allow me to become king some day.

WOOD. No matter how many people you have to kill along the way?

RICHARD. And do you think that is wrong, Mr. Wood? Your problem is that you feel inclined to define your world in terms of good and evil. I am beyond such prosaic terms. I am evil. And I am good at it. I want to be king, Wood. It's all I ever dream about. It's all I ever wanted. What do you want, Wood?

WOOD. Why should I tell you?

RICHARD. Because I have already killed one man who refused to tell me where the knife was.

WOOD. And how should I know?

RICHARD. You're the one who called the meeting at St. Mark's. And in addition you have been seen with a woman who I know to have once had possession of the knife.

WOOD. What's so important about that friggin' knife?

RICHARD. You mean you do not know? Did not Iago tell you? My dear Iago, how discourteous to keep someone in the dark so long.

IAGO. Apologies, my lord.

RICHARD. What do you know of the Knights of Malta, Mr. Wood?

WOOD. They are one of the most powerful knightly orders in the world.

RICHARD. And sadly one of the most pious. But what I meant was; what do you know of their history?

WOOD. History was never one of my best subjects.

RICHARD. In order to shape history, one must know history. Allow me to enlighten you. The Knights of Saint John arrived on Malta in 1530 after being driven from Rhodes by the Turks. The next thirty years were devoted to building defenses and fortresses in expectation of an attack by the Turks. In 1565 the attack finally came as the Grand Turk set an entire fleet and thousands of troops against that single order of knights. But the Knights of Malta were victorious. Do you know why?

WOOD. Because they were lucky?

RICHARD. Partially. But the Knights had another advantage. A year before the siege began, a merchant of Venice landed on Malta and warned them of the impending attack. To honor this merchant, the Knights presented him with a bejeweled dagger bearing the Maltese cross on the blade.

WOOD. So why does everybody want it?

RICHARD. Accompanying the knife was the promise that if the merchant or any of descendants ever required the assistance of the Maltese Knights, they had but to present the blade and the Knights would provide an army.

WOOD. They promised that?

RICHARD. They swore to it. It was a secret, of course. But when the merchant's only son married into a family as large as the Montagues... Well, secrets become a little harder to keep.

WOOD. And what do you need an army for?

RICHARD. I have ambitions.

WOOD. And why was my partner killed?

RICHARD. (*smiles in* **CATESBY**'s *direction*) I don't know. The bodkin disappeared from the Montague vaults a year ago, shortly after my dear Iago joined my company. I mean to have that knife, Mr. Wood. It represents a great power to me.

CATESBY. Where is the Maltese Bodkin?

WOOD. I don't know.

RICHARD. Come now, Wood. I am not a fool and I do not appreciate being treated as one.

WOOD. It was in my office last night. It was gone when I arrived this morning.

RICHARD. Then why did you call the meeting at St. Mark's.

WOOD. I was hoping to attract the guy who took it. It's evidence in a double murder.

RICHARD. A *double* murder? I am only aware of one. But then it is so hard to keep track of them all. Catesby. (**CATESBY** *steps forward*) Go you and search Mr. Wood's office.

(**CATESBY** *goes to exit, but then pauses having forgotten what his objective is.*)

IAGO (*aside to* **CATESBY**) The Maltese Bodkin.

(*The light dawns and* **CATESBY** *exits.*)

RICHARD. I am disappointed in you, Mr. Wood.

WOOD. I'm telling the truth.

RICHARD. Which is what disappoints me. A lie would lead to further conversation, but I fear this truth shall end all conversation. Iago! Caesario!

(**IAGO** *steps forward to take orders. As does the figure who has remained hidden in the shadows. The man whom* **RICHARD** *calls Caesario is none other than* **VIOLA** *dressed in men's clothing.*)

RICHARD (*addressing* **VIOLA**) My good Caesario. I leave it in thy hands to dispose of this morsel.

IAGO. And I, my good and gracious royal lion of destiny?

RICHARD. Just help Caesario. I don't respond to flattery, Iago. I recognize my short comings too well to accept a compliment. Caesario. You know thy task.

VIOLA. Aye, my lord.

RICHARD. Farewell, Mr. Wood. I fear we shall not meet again. Neither in this life nor the next.

(**RICHARD** *exits.* **VIOLA** *steps forward.* **WOOD** *has but an instant to register her identity.*)

WOOD. Miss da-

(**IAGO** *knocks him out once more. The lights black out just as* **WOOD** *does.*)

(*BLACK OUT*)

Day 4

Scene Five

WOOD (*addressing the audience*) Knock, knock, knock. A few knock to the head are all part of the P.I. game. This one should have been the Big Sleep. Instead I woke up in a gutter in Eastcheap. With Donalbain gone, so was my pipeline to the noble houses. But maybe the answers I needed were waiting for me. Back at the bottom of Boar's Head.

(*Lights go out on* **WOOD** *and then come up on the dank and murky cellar of the Boar's Head Tavern. There is a cold silence only broken by the sound of dripping water. Then there are descending footsteps.* **QUICKLY** *holds a lantern as she guides* **WOOD** *down the stairs.*)

QUICKLY. 'Ere. Come this way, Woody. Only a few more steps.

WOOD. Geez, Nell. Didn't you give 'em any light?

QUICKLY. I gave them plenty of lantern light. But they have a ways of blowing them out when they hears someone's coming. I think they're still afraid of being executed.

WOOD. Didn't you tell them they were safe?

QUICKLY. Aye. But being locked in a cellar for a week seems to have dampened their belief in other people's good nature.

(*Two figures can be dimly seen in the half light. They are dressed in an identical fashion. Their dirty and well worn clothing was at one time the highest of noble fashion, but days trapped in the dark cellar have worn down both fashionability and sanity. They mutter back and forth.*)

WOOD. What are they doing?

QUICKLY. I don't know. Keeps them occupied.

FIRST VOICE. Why are we here?

SECOND VOICE. How did we get here?

FIRST VOICE. What is the reason?

SECOND VOICE. What is the purpose?

FIRST VOICE. Foul! No synonyms! My point!

SECOND VOICE. Did that count?

FIRST VOICE. Why shouldn't it?

SECOND VOICE. Is that fair?

FIRST VOICE. Is anything fair?

SECOND VOICE. Why should it be?

FIRST VOICE. Why should you care?

SECOND VOICE/WOOD. What going on?

FIRST VOICE/QUICKLY. What do you mean?

SECOND VOICE. Is this a game?

FIRST VOICE/QUICKLY. What did you say?

WOOD. Is this game?

FIRST VOICE. Foul! No repetition! Three-Love, game to me!

SECOND VOICE. I'm still winning sixty four games to thirty.

FIRST VOICE. Oh, no you're not.

WOOD. Nell?

QUICKLY. Yes, Woody?

WOOD. I think they've been locked up too long.

(**WOOD** *and* **QUICKLY** *approach the two figures.*)

QUICKLY. Come out you two.

FIRST VOICE. Who's there?

QUICKLY. It's only Nell.

SECOND VOICE. Who's with you?

QUICKLY. It's just Woody. Birnam Wood. Remember? He brought you here.

FIRST VOICE. Prove it.

SECOND VOICE. We must be sure.

FIRST VOICE. We're in danger…

QUICKLY. No you're not.

SECOND VOICE. We're to be executed.

QUICKLY. No you're not. Tell them, Woody.

WOOD. You're not going to be killed.

FIRST VOICE. There was a letter…

SECOND VOICE. We brought a letter…

FIRST VOICE. A letter that demanded the immediate execution –

SECOND VOICE. Upon delivery the deaths of –

(**QUICKLY** *lights a candle, bathing the scene in feeble light. We see the two ferrety men huddled together in fear.*)

FIRST VOICE (ROSENCRANTZ) – of Rosencrantz and gentle Guildenstern.

SECOND VOICE (GUILDENSTERN) – of Guildenstern and gentle Rosencrantz.

QUICKLY. There you are, lads. Light to see by.

ROSENCRANTZ. Light to see by…

GUILDENSTERN. Or light to be seen by.

(*They whimper.*)

QUICKLY. They're addled I think, Woody.

WOOD. Rosencrantz.

GUILDENSTERN. That's he.

ROSENCRANTZ. That's me.

WOOD. Guildenstern.

ROSENCRANTZ. The other.

GUILDENSTERN. 'Tis I.

WOOD. I need information.

ROSENCRANTZ. Were we not to be killed?

GUILDENSTERN. Are we to be killed?

WOOD. No. You're not prisoners. You're here for your own safety.

ROSENCRANTZ. We brought a letter…

GUILDENSTERN. …to the English king.

WOOD. And he knew it was a forgery. His name was misspelled. He asked me to put you in a safe place and then sent me to Denmark to find out what was going on.

ROSENCRANTZ. What went on?

WOOD. A dismal sight. The affairs I brought arrived too late. The ears were senseless that would give me hearing. The report of the commandment fulfilled was undeliv'red. All that I said, to protect the fraud, was Rosencrantz and Guildenstern were dead. (*through the speech* **WOOD***'s speaking voice has taken on Shakespearean tone and cadence.*)

nice

QUICKLY. A nice speech, Woody.

WOOD. I can speak the lingo when I need to. Any way, I stayed in Denmark a while. But I never found out who wanted you dead. I have a report to give to the King. Once he reads it, you'll be free.

ROSENCRANTZ. You've been back a week.

GUILDENSTERN. Why has not your report been made?

WOOD. My partner was killed while I was gone.

ROSENCRANTZ. Better he than noble Guildenstern-

GUILDENSTERN. – or virtuous Rosencrantz.

WOOD. You want out?

GUILDENSTERN. Of course.

ROSENCRANTZ. We do!

WOOD. Then I want some information. Tell me what I need to know and I'll deliver my report.

ROSENCRANTZ. Then ask –

GUILDENSTERN. – and we will answer –

ROSENCRANTZ. – if we can.

WOOD. What do you know about Scotland?

GUILDENSTERN. It's cold –

ROSENCRANTZ. – and wet –

GUILDENSTERN. – and filled with Scotsmen.

QUICKLY. I coulda told you that.

WOOD. What about the kings?

ROSENCRANTZ. Of Scotland?

WOOD. Yes.

GUILDENSTERN. Dangerous –

ROSENCRANTZ. – to be king –

GUILDENSTERN. – in Scotland.

WOOD. Why?

ROSENCRANTZ. There are always others who wish to be king –

GUILDENSTERN. – in warlike Scotland –

ROSENCRANTZ. – where knives are plenty –

GUILDENSTERN. – and people kill for what they wish. The latest king –

ROSENCRANTZ. Malcolm.

GUILDENSTERN. – his father –

ROSENCRANTZ. Duncan.

GULIDENSTERN. – was a king.

ROSENCRANTZ. A murdered king.

QUICKLY. Sounds like a right nice place.

ROSENCRANTZ. Can we go now?

GUILDENSTERN. We gave you news.

WOOD. Did Malcolm kill him?

ROSENCRANTZ. Who?

WOOD. The king.

QUICKLY. His dad?

WOOD. Yes.

GUILDENSTERN. No.

WOOD. Then who did?

ROSENCRANTZ. What?

WOOD. Killed the king. King Duncan, Malcolm's father.

GUILDENSTERN. Another.

ROSENCRANTZ. A man who's thane.

QUICKLY. As opposed to inthane?

WOOD. Quiet.

QUICKLY. Sorry.

WOOD. So the king was killed by...

ROSENCRANTZ. The thane of Glamis.

GUILDENSTERN. The thane of Cawdor.

ROSENCRANTZ. Both.

WOOD. Two men?

ROSENCRANTZ. One man –

GUILDENSTERN. – with two titles –

ROSENCRANTZ. – and a wife.

GUILDENSTERN. And what a wife.

WOOD. So why did the thane kill the king?

ROSENCRANTZ. Because he –

GUILDENSTERN. The thane.

ROSENCRANTZ. – had a wife –

GUILDENSTERN. Ambitious wife.

ROSENCRANTZ. – who pushed him on.

QUICKLY. That's it. Blame the woman.

GUILDENSTERN. And there was a prophecy… *[handwritten: jump backward]*

WOOD. A prophecy?

ROSENCRANTZ/GUILDENSTERN. A prophecy. *[handwritten: gather together]*

ROSENCRANTZ. Made by <u>witches</u> – *[handwritten: act]*

GUILDENSTERN. – that he –

ROSENCRANTZ. The thane. *[handwritten: → Push Dan forward]*

GUILDENSTERN. – would be king. *[handwritten: ⇒ bows]*

WOOD. Where is this guy now?

ROSENCRANTZ. He's dead. *[handwritten: — laying on the ground]*

GUILDENSTERN. Thank heaven. *[handwritten: — crosses self]*

ROSENCRANTZ. Killed on the field of battle. *[handwritten: — jumps up]*

GUILDENSTERN. Beheaded – *[handwritten: — cut motion on Dan]*

QUICKLY. Yech.

ROSENCRANTZ. – and betrayed. *[handwritten: — stab Dan in back]*

WOOD. And the wife?

GUILDENSTERN. She died before. *[handwritten: — one side of Mel]*

ROSENCRANTZ. She went inthane. *[handwritten: — other side]*

[handwritten left margin: Dan make sure you guys down to listen to them to]

> (**ROSENCRANTZ** *and* **QUICKLY** *share a laugh.* **WOOD**
> *and* **GUILDENSTERN** *look on disapprovingly.*)

ROSENCRANTZ/QUICKLY. Sorry.

GUILDENSTERN. She killed herself – *[handwritten: — matter of fact]*

ROSENCRANTZ. – thrown from the battlements – *[handwritten: — push Mel for.]*

GUILDENSTERN. – as the armies that would kill her husband

[handwritten: march onward to Wood]

marched upon the castle.

WOOD. The name? The name of the thane? *[handwritten: — hesitation on name, push Dan forward]*

ROSENCRANTZ. He was MacBeth.

GUILDENSTERN. Killed by MacDuff. *[handwritten: — step]*

ROSENCRANTZ. Succeeded by Malcolm. *[handwritten: — step forward]*

GUILDENSTERN. Who rules today. *[handwritten: — bows to Rose.]*

(**WOOD** *mulls this over.*)

QUICKLY. That Malcolm. He's Donalbain's brother, right? *[handwritten: pull Wood away, step aside]*

WOOD. Yeah.

QUICKLY. If he...

WOOD. Got worried about Donny?

QUICKLY. Could he have...

WOOD. Killed Donny?

ROSENCRANTZ/GUILDENSTERN. Yes. *[handwritten: — listening in]*

ROSENCRANTZ. That's the way things are done in warlike Scotland –

GUILDENSTERN. – where things are cold and wet –

ROSENCRANTZ. – and knives are plenty.

GUILDENSTERN. Is that all you wanted to know?

ROSENCRANTZ. Will you deliver your report?

GUILDENSTERN. So we can leave?

WOOD. Thanks, boys. You've been a help. Come on, Nell. (*aside to* **NELL**) Let the poor schmucks out. The King has had the report for a week. I doubt he'll care one way or another.

QUICKLY. Aye. I'll let them out. They'll be happy. You don't look too pleased though. Is this case of yours too difficult for ye?

WOOD. No. I think I got a handle on it now. And it's a mess. A royal, bloody mess. And it looks like I've been appointed the guy to clean up.

(**WOOD** *exits.* **QUICKLY** *goes down to give the news to* **ROSENCRANTZ** *and* **GUILDENSTERN** *the news. They jump at her unexpected arrival.*) *[handwritten: Make sure you go back Nell. R+G begin process over again.]*

(*BLACK OUT*)

Scene Six

(*The saxophone music transitions into another* **WOOD** *monologue.*)

WOOD. There was guy who once said all the world's a stage and everybody's just a bunch of actors. Well, if that was true I was finally gettin' in step with this particular production. The plot was still a little murky, but I was beginning to understand the casting. And somewhere between a missing brother, a hunchbacked Duke, a dangerous dame who dressed in guy's clothing and a bunch o' Venetians was the author of this little melodrama.

(*The scene shifts back to the office where the morning is breaking.* **WOOD** *is seated behind his desk reading his Shakespeare as* **CHARLOTTE** *enters ready for the day's work. She is startled by* **WOOD**'s *unexpected presence. She gives a small scream of surprise.*)

CHARLOTTE. Not again. If this keeps up I'm going to have to start showing up on time. You okay?

WOOD. Just wonderin' why I'm still alive.

CHARLOTTE. Well, if it's any comfort I'm glad you're still around. I hid the knife.

WOOD. Did you ever read this stuff?

CHARLOTTE. No.

WOOD. Listen. Does this make any sense to you? "When shall we three meet again? In thunder, lightning or in rain. When the hurly-burly's done. When the battle's lost and won. That will be ere the set of sun. Where the place? Upon the heath."

CHARLOTTE. Sounds like a weather report. Whatchu reading that for?

WOOD. Research. And I'm learning plenty.

CHARLOTTE. Going to look for that brother today?

WOOD. I think'd be safer if he wasn't found. Other than that, I think I've got this case halfway cracked.

CHARLOTTE. Do you know who killed Mr. Heath?

WOOD. Not yet.

CHARLOTTE. And what about our client?

WOOD. I'm expecting our client to show up today. She's got a lot of explaining to do.

(*The office door opens and* **VIOLA** *stands framed in the doorway. She wears a sultry gown and her attitude matches her fashion statement.*)

VIOLA. Forgiveth please my entry, sir, without thy invitation. But sad to say, your menial was not tending to her station. →make this more derrogatory

WOOD. Sure, doll face. Charlotte was just leaving. (*to* **CHARLOTTE**) By the way, I'll be wanting that item I gave you delivered here tomorrow morning at ten o'clock.

CHARLOTTE. Gotcha. (*gives a dirty look to* **VIOLA** *as she exits*)

WOOD. So, what do you have to say for yourself, Miss Viola? Or is it Mr. Caesario?

VIOLA. Thou need not be so intemperate, Mr. Wood. I have come to thee on my accord to offer explanation.

WOOD. I'm listening.

VIOLA. Thou art curious as to my attendance upon the Duke.

WOOD. Good place to start.

VIOLA. 'Tis a simple enough account.

WOOD. I'll bet.

VIOLA. It concerns my brother.

WOOD. That's what I thought you'd say.

VIOLA. I am desperate, Mr. Wood. I wouldst do anything to find him. 'Tis well known the Duke of Gloucester hath satellites in every dastard corner of the capital. Through my father's friends among the dockside smugglers, I did obtain an audience with the Duke Richard. And taking the raiment of a boy did join the villain's band as the masque Caesario.

WOOD. Why didn't you tell me?

VIOLA. Through ignorance I hoped to spare thee.

WOOD. So, you were thinking of me.

VIOLA. I think on thee muchly.

WOOD. So. Did you get any more information on your brother?

VIOLA. No. I am at my wit's end.

WOOD. What about the Duke?

VIOLA. He cares not for anything save the crown of England. He knew not of my brother as I was sorry to discover. Oh, Mr. Wood, where is Sebastian?

WOOD. Where do you think?

VIOLA (*closing in on* **WOOD**) I know not. He may be in straits perilous. Thou must save him and through him I.

WOOD. You're very persuasive. I'll give you that.

VIOLA. What art thou saying? I have been true to thee.

WOOD. Sorry. I woke up this morning with a bit of a headache.

VIOLA. Thou wert to be dead, you know.

WOOD. Then why wert I?

VIOLA. I saved thy life!

WOOD. And just how did you do that?

VIOLA. As thou hast spoken, I can be very persuasive if needs be. I convinced the man Iago to spare thee. He likes me.

WOOD. You?

VIOLA. Him.

WOOD. Caesario?

VIOLA. Yes.

WOOD. Oh. (*pause*) I know he's willing to spare a life for you. What about the flipside?

VIOLA. What doth thou say?

WOOD. Do you think he's willing to kill for you?

VIOLA. Who would I desire death of?

WOOD. I'm asking the questions.

VIOLA. Thou wouldst bind and baiteth me when I have e'er been true to thee. 'Twas I alone who rescued thy mortality with markèd threat to my vitality. The Duke, curse him, will seek me now.

WOOD. You should be okay. He'll be looking for some kid named Caesario. Unless he knows who you really are.

VIOLA (*snapping*) No one knows who I really am! (*pause, recovering her calm*) Oh, Mr. Wood. Thou must aid me. I am a solitary on foreign shores and must needs gather help where I may. Thou art my only hope. My sole comfort.

WOOD. (*beat*) Oh, you're good. Really good.

VIOLA. What doth thou sayest?

WOOD. Well, if I'm gonna find your brother then I better get started. And if you're so concerned about the Duke maybe you should go back to that hotel room of yours and lay low for a while.

(**WOOD** *holds the door for her.*)

VIOLA. I am so glad that thou wouldst continue to work on my behalf. I know thou wilt find my brother. I have such confidence in thee.

(*They close in a clinch and kiss, a steamy Bogart/Bacall kind of kiss. They come up for air and descend again. They finally, softly, reluctantly part lips. There is a pause.*)

VIOLA (*softly*) By the by… Where is the knife?

WOOD. It's… safe.

VIOLA. I… see.

(*A downcast* **CHARLOTTE** *enters.*)

CHARLOTTE. Someone to see you, boss.

WOOD. That's okay, Charlotte. Miss da…

CHARLOTTE. Messaline?

WOOD. Yeah. …was just leaving.

VIOLA (*seductively*) 'Til common purpose draw us to other.

(*As* **VIOLA** *exits she shoots a significant glance in* **CHARLOTTE**'s *direction.* **CHARLOTTE** *watches her go. Pause.*)

WOOD. Charlotte.

CHARLOTTE. What?

WOOD. Who's here?

CHARLOTTE. Oh. A Mr. Mercutio to see you.

WOOD. Damn. What does he want? Send him in.

> (**CHARLOTTE** *exits while* **WOOD** *returns to his desk. In a moment she returns with* **MERCUTIO**.)

MERCUTIO. Why was that woman here?

WOOD. She's my client.

> (**CHARLOTTE** *exits.*)

MERCUTIO. Yo her evils I did caution thee.

WOOD. Evil and I are on a first name basis. How can I be of service to you?

MERCUTIO. The question should be the reverse. There is a debt between us…

WOOD. Let's forget the whole thing.

MERCUTIO. I owe thee a service.

WOOD. Well, I don't play tennis so you're outta luck.

MERCUTIO. I have found the man that thou art looking for.

WOOD. What?

MERCUTIO. The man thou callest Sebastian.

WOOD. Damn. (*beat*) Where is he?

MERCUTIO. He is a guest of the Lord Mayor of London.

WOOD. Pretty swell digs.

MERCUTIO. I have secured thy passage into the manor house. The household guards are cheaply bought and a round of ale has ensured thy unobstructed entry.

WOOD. Okay. I'm going. By myself.

MERCUTIO. But I still may be of-

WOOD. Thanks, Murray. I'll catch you later.

MERCUTIO. But –

> (**WOOD** *exits.* **MERCUTIO** *is alone. He stands confused for a moment, then trying to make the most of the opportunity he moves to the desk. He starts searching* **WOOD**'s *drawers when…*)

WOOD (*re-entering*) Get outta my office.

> (*BLACK OUT*)

FIX THIS!!!...

Scene Seven

(*Night. Interior of the Lord Mayor's manor. A young man sits reading. He is a handsome, attentive man with manners suggesting royalty. This is* **SEBASTIAN**. **WOOD** *enters silently behind* **SEBASTIAN**, *who is apparently unaware of his presence. As* **WOOD** *closes in*, **SEBASTIAN** *addresses him without looking up from the book.*)

SEBASTIAN. Mr. Wood.

(**WOOD** *is caught off guard, but retains his composure.*)

WOOD. I don't believe we've met.

SEBASTIAN. You are not unknown to me, Mr. Wood.

WOOD. I'm not sure I like that. You must be… Sebastian?

SEBASTIAN. It's the name I've been using in London.

Sebastian - give me more of a hidden accent

WOOD. Then it's not your real name?

sit

SEBASTIAN. Hardly.

motion to sit

WOOD. So what do I call you?

SEBASTIAN. You can call me Sebastian.

WOOD. Okay.

SEBASTIAN. I'm not certain what to make of you, Mr. Wood. You present a certain danger to me that I'm not sure even you are aware of.

WOOD. I'm just trying to find you.

SEBASTIAN. Being found could be the death of me.

WOOD. I'm working for your sister.

SEBASTIAN. She's not my sister.

WOOD. I didn't think so.

SEBASTIAN. Good day, Mr. Wood. *— stands up to leave*

(**SEBASTIAN** *pointedly returns to his reading.* **WOOD** *turns to go, then pauses. He turns back to the lad.*)

WOOD. You're from Scotland, aren't you?

SEBASTIAN (*startled*) I thought I lost my accent.

WOOD. You're the kid aren't you? The one in the prophecy.

Stand up

SEBASTIAN. You know a great deal more than I suspected, Mr. Wood. I've underestimated you.

WOOD. Everyone does.

SEBASTIAN. Have you told her where I am?

WOOD. I haven't told anything to Miss da Messaline.

SEBASTIAN. Da Messaline? Is that the name she's using now?

WOOD. She doesn't know. Yet.

stand up SEBASTIAN. But she will. She's the reason I've been in hiding all these years. She wants to kill me.

WOOD. She's capable of that?

SEBASTIAN. And much more.

WOOD. Why would she want to kill you?

SEBASTIAN. Revenge. She wants to confound the prophecy. She blames me, I think, for a part in her downfall. I was fortunate to flee with my life.

WOOD. And your father?

SEBASTIAN. Murdered.

WOOD. Sorry. What's her connection to the Maltese Bodkin?

slow this down SEBASTIAN. I've never heard of it. What is it?

WOOD. It's what killed my partner.

SEBASTIAN. Is it revenge that drives thee, Wood? Take care. Vengeance is a cruel and fickle hound that will scar its master as it devours its prey.

WOOD. Who are you?

SEBASTIAN. My name is Fleance.

WOOD. Fleance? And who is Miss da Messaline?

SEBASTIAN. Why she is –

(CATESBY *suddenly enters, armed with a dagger.*)

CATESBY. Wood!

SEBASTIAN. You've been followed, Wood. (*turns to exit*)

WOOD. Wait! Kid!

(WOOD *tries to stop* SEBASTIAN *but is shrugged*

off. **SEBASTIAN** *exits quickly.* **CATESBY** *closes in on* **WOOD**.)

CATESBY. Where is the Maltese Bodkin?

WOOD. What's it to you? → *More Bogart*

CATESBY. The bodkin will help the Duke become king, Mr. Wood. And when he becomes king, then I will become a duke, Mr. Wood. I want to be a duke, Mr. Wood.

WOOD. We all have our dreams.

(**CATESBY** *lunges with his knife and* **WOOD** *dodges. When* **WOOD** *draws his gun* **CATESBY** *knocks it out of his hand.* **CATESBY** *has the upper hand and although* **WOOD** *puts up a good fight, he is hopelessly outclassed. In the end* **WOOD** *finds himself trapped under* **CATESBY**'s *knife.*)

CATESBY. I have already stabbed one man through the back, Mr. Wood. I shall have no trouble doing the same for you.

(**CATESBY** *is about to deliver the killing blow when a shot rings out.* **CATESBY** *is thrown forward to the ground. As* **WOOD** *struggles to his feet* **VIOLA** *steps forward with* **WOOD**'s *pistol still smoking in her hand.*)

Needs Revision

VIOLA. Interesting device. Saves time.

WOOD. Gimme that. (*grabs the gun*) Before you hurt someone with it.

VIOLA. Is he dead?

WOOD. Nah. You just winged him.

VIOLA. He is a danger to thee.

WOOD. Him and everyone else.

VIOLA. He would slay thee.

WOOD. What's your point?

VIOLA. Wilt thou kill him?

WOOD. What?

VIOLA. If thou would let the villain live he would but hunt thee down again. Take action now, thou must know how to bring the hunter's end.

WOOD. I ain't no killer.

VIOLA. No one will know.

WOOD. You'll know.

VIOLA. I will not tell.

WOOD. I'll know.

VIOLA. I can ease thy conscience.

WOOD. I'll bet.

VIOLA. He is a fiend and shall not be missed if thou wouldst do as thou desirest.

WOOD. You think?

VIOLA. I do.

WOOD. I see.

VIOLA. 'Tis what he would do if thou wert lying there.

WOOD. You're right.

VIOLA. Revenge is fit and sweet. 'Tis thy reward and thou must taste it while thou mayest.

WOOD. Yeah.

VIOLA. Use the weapon.

WOOD. No.

VIOLA. The dagger then.

WOOD. I won't.

VIOLA. Then give it unto me. The sleeping are but as pictures. 'Tis the eye of childhood that fears the fallen foe.

WOOD. No.

VIOLA. O my heart, canst thou not find fire in a dagger's gleam? The lesson's there for those who dare-

WOOD. Things aren't always what they seem.

VIOLA. (*beat*) If apprehension be thy fear then I thy alibi shall be. I shall say we were enjoined. At the Dolphin. In Room Three.

WOOD. I don't think any sane man would let themselves be alone with you. How did you find me?

VIOLA. I followed thee from thy office. I slipped slyly past the guards and found thee here in combat. Why art thou here? Hast thou my brother found?

WOOD. Nah. I was quizzin' the Mayor's staff.

VIOLA. I. See.

WOOD. Come to the office tomorrow morning at ten.

VIOLA. 'Til then.

(**VIOLA** *exits.* **WOOD** *carefully watches her go. He then turns his attention to* **CATESBY** *and slaps him awake. He keeps his gun pointed at the villain.*)

WOOD. Listen here, Laughing Boy. You go tell the Duke that if he wants more information on the bodkin, I'll be spilling the beans at my office ten o'clock tomorrow morning. Comprende? Now beat it.

(**CATESBY** *hurriedly exits holding his wounded arm.*)

(*FADE OUT*)

[handwritten: Make sure you're on one knee — not hovering]

Scene Eight

(*It is morning.* **WOOD** *is seated behind the desk reading his Shakespeare book.*)

WOOD. "Tomorrow and tomorrow and tomorrow, creeps in this petty pace from day to day." (*suddenly struck by a thought*) No. (*reconsiders*) Maybe.

(**WOOD** *dives back into the book. Totally engrossed he does not see the office door silently open.* **IAGO** *enters. Seeing the unwary* **WOOD***, he draws his sword and advances on him. He is nearly upon his victim when* **WOOD** *spins in his chair with pistol drawn. Looking down the barrel of the gun* **IAGO** *freezes. He looks at the gun. Pause.*)

IAGO. You sent for me?

WOOD. Siddown.

(**IAGO** *quickly sheaths his weapon and sits heavily in the client's chair.*)

IAGO. A proper host would put away his weapon.

WOOD. I ain't a proper host.

IAGO. The Duke sent me.

WOOD. That's his problem. Just be quiet and wait. There are others coming.

IAGO. Others? What others?

WOOD. Didn't I tell you to be quiet?

IAGO. Ah yes. So you did. Foolish I was to ask. Sorry, Forgot myself. I will not speak again. No more. Sh.

WOOD. Good boy. And by the way, I know all about what you pulled in that Othello caper. You dirty rat.

(**CHARLOTTE** *enters.*)

CHARLOTTE. What is this? Come early to work week?

WOOD. Charlotte, meet Iago.

IAGO. I am very –

WOOD. Sit!

IAGO. Sorry.

WOOD. Iago works for the Duke.

CHARLOTTE. No kiddin'? What's he doin' here?

WOOD. He's here to see me solve this case.

IAGO. I am? I am.

CHARLOTTE. You solved the case? Then who – ?

FANG (*entering*) Is that what this is about, Wood? I told you that case was closed.

WOOD. A crime has been committed, Fang.

FANG. Ooh. What crime, Wood? An arson perhaps? 'Bout 'ere that would be an act of the public good.

WOOD. I didn't ask your opinion, you blown-up bumbling bobby, just your presence. I'm going to be handing you Archie's killer on a silver platter and if you have half a brain you'll stand there quiet with your cuffs at hand.

FANG. Now see 'ere, Wood. I am an officer of the crown and I expect nothin' but respect for the badge I wear.

WOOD. Oh, I respect the badge. It's what's pinned to it I find disagreeable.

IAGO. If you're talking privately, perhaps I should go?

WOOD/FANG. Siddown!

IAGO. Sorry.

FANG. I'm not at your beck and call, Wood. I'm a sergeant of the guard and I will not be summoned up like a two penny street harlot.

WOOD. A man knows his own price.

FANG. That's it. I'm swearing a warrant 'gainst you, Wood. Disrespect. Talking back to an officer of the law. I'll 'ave you up on charges.

(**FANG** *is striding towards the door when* **VIOLA** *abruptly steps into the doorway blocking his exit.* **FANG** *freezes.*)

VIOLA. Mr. Wood. Am I too early?

WOOD. Not at all, Miss da Messaline. Come right in. I'm sure Mr. Iago won't mind giving up his seat.

VIOLA. Thank you.

(**VIOLA** *floats into the chair.* **FANG** *can't take his eyes* *off her.*)

WOOD. You still here, Fang? I thought you were going.

FANG. Ahem. Well. I thought I might be staying a while. Only to take note of your further offenses against the crown, you understand.

WOOD. Yeah. I understand.

FANG (*hovering over* **VIOLA** *like a bad smell*) Hello. I'm a sergeant of the guard. My name is Fang.

VIOLA. You have my sympathy.

WOOD (*whispering to* **CHARLOTTE**) You have the Mac-Guffin?

CHARLOTTE. What? Oh yeah. It's in my handbag.

WOOD. Good. I'll need it after my last guest arrives.

MERCUTIO (*entering*) Good lord, Wood. Hast thou taken in boarders?

WOOD (*to* **CHARLOTTE**) Stand by.

MERCUTIO. Mr. Wood. I have come in response to thy request. Ten o'clock thou didst say and ten o'clock it is.

VIOLA. Hast thou summoned us to produce my brother?

IAGO. Your brother? You lie a falseness. A brother…

FANG. Quiet you. Poor lady. Have you lost your brother?

MERCUTIO. She has not. She is after the Maltese Bodkin. It's is the Montagues' –

IAGO. It is the Duke's –

FANG. Now, I told you to be –

MERCUTIO. My quest –

(**WOOD** *fires his gun into the air.*)

WOOD. Will everyone be quiet?

VIOLA. I thank thee, Mr. Wood.

WOOD. Including you. For the last few days I've been run around, knocked on the head, held by criminals and been threatened with various sorts of bodily harm. And all for one thing.

MERCUTIO. The knife.

VIOLA. My brother.

WOOD. My partner. The rest of it doesn't matter.

CHARLOTTE. But what about the knife?

VIOLA. 'Tis the weapon that killed Archie Heath.

FANG. What?

IAGO. Where is it?

FANG. That's evidence.

MERCUTIO. 'Tis my obligation. It is important –

WOOD. The only important thing is finding Archie's killer.

CHARLOTTE. Who was it? Who killed him? Who stabbed Archie?

WOOD. Those are two different questions, Charlotte. But I'll start with who stabbed Archie.

VIOLA. It was Sir William Catesby.

WOOD. What makes you say that?

VIOLA. Last night he spoke of stabbing a man in the back. The very method by which Mr. Heath was killed.

WOOD. Yeah. Catesby stabbed Archie. But the question is why. Archie was working on a case for Miss da Messaline here. Looking for her brother. Sebastian. She said she pulled the bodkin out of Archie's body. Then she gave it to me in order to ensure my cooperation.

MERCUTIO. I saw her in the alley.

WOOD. She hired me to finish Archie's case.

CHARLOTTE. And what about her brother?

WOOD. Gone. Safe.

VIOLA. Where is he?

WOOD. The biggest problem with this case was the knife. Everybody wanted it. Murray wanted it because he was honor bound to send it back home.

MERCUTIO. I will do anything to get it back.

IAGO. Anything?

WOOD. And the Duke wanted it because it would bring the Knights of Saint John on to his side. Isn't that right?

IAGO. Of course.

WOOD. It was Richard was arranged for the bodkin to be

stolen from the Montagues. Wasn't it, Iago?

IAGO. Indeed. I was the one who did so. When fleeing Cyprus, the site of a simple misunderstanding which led to my arrest, I was contacted. By certain criminals I was, who smuggled me out. So I set my course for England, stopping only long enough to rob the foolish Montagues.

MERCUTIO. THIEF!!

(**IAGO** *and* **MERCUTIO** *attempt to cross swords.* **WOOD** *warns them back with his gun.*)

WOOD (*shaking his head*) Italians. But you lost the knife.

IAGO. Stolen from me it was. In Dover.

WOOD. Obviously it had to be an inside job. Only a few people knew of the knife's significance.

CHARLOTTE. I got it! It was Catesby. He works for the Duke and woulda known about the knife.

WOOD. Nah. Catesby stabbed Archie. He stabbed him and knew the knife was special. But he wasn't the one who stole it from Iago. Why would he leave the knife in Archie's back if he knew how special it was? And why did he kill Archie in the first place?

FANG. I don't know.

WOOD. Richard told me he had already had one man killed because he thought he had the knife. That man was Archie.

FANG. Wait a minute. Why would Catesby think that Heath had the knife when he killed him with the very same knife?

WOOD. Obviously Catesby didn't have the knife. Murray here actually saw Miss da Messaline pull a knife form Archie's body. And although the alley was dark it was still light enough to see clearly. He saw her, but he didn't see the Maltese Bodkin.

MERCUTIO. 'Tis true. The knife I saw her take was but an ordinary dagger.

WOOD. Catesby killed Archie because he knew that Archie was working for the person who actually had the knife.

When Archie was killed that person knew the knife was too hot to hold and so had to put in some place safe. And what safer place could there be than in the hands of some poor sap who was told it was a vital clue in his friend's murder?

VIOLA. I underestimated you, Mr. Wood.

WOOD. Everybody does. You made up the story about pulling the bodkin from Archie's body. You had it all along. It was you who stole the knife from Iago in the guise of one of the Duke's men. Isn't that right, Caesario?

IAGO. You?

WOOD. The bodkin was never used in the murder. When you gave it to me it was as clean as the day it was made. The only knicks on it came from Donalbain. Archie was killed because he was working for you. You set him up to be your fall guy. You killed Archie as surely as if you pushed the knife in yourself.

FANG. That's a pretty flimsy connection for a murder charge, Wood.

MERCUTIO. And why would she want the bodkin?

WOOD. Revenge. You met Donalbain in my office. Later that nigh he was dead. Killed by the Maltese Bodkin. But only three people saw where I put the knife. Donalbain, myself and you.

CHARLOTTE. She killed Donny?

IAGO. Of course she did.

FANG. Why?

WOOD. Because she was afraid of being recognized. She didn't bother to bring out her brother's picture until Donny was out of the room. Something that important you'd figure she's show first thing. But why would Donny be any danger unless he could recognize the kid in the picture. And if he knew the kid, he'd know the lady.

FANG. Then who is she?

WOOD. A former queen who wants revenge on the people who killed her husband. People whose revenge she escaped only after faking her own death. She needs the bodkin in order to defeat the armies of Scotland. But it all would have been in vain if the son of prophecy was still alive. You ain't Caesario. Or Viola. I know who you really are. Lady MacBeth.

(*gasps and uproar*)

VIOLA (*exploding*) Quiet. (*then composing herself*) Very good, Birnam Wood. I came close to my goal though. Pity about the boy.

WOOD. Sebastian.

VIOLA. Fleance. Son of Banquo. One of the few victims to escape my husband's grasp.

WOOD. A father to a line of kings.

VIOLA. I say thee nay, sir. He rose nearly to my bait. I could but smell his blood within the Mayor's estate.

WOOD. He'll be free of you now.

VIOLA. Mayhap. But he knows fear. As all in Scotland would have know, if I and all the Maltese knights had ridden into Scone.

MERCUTIO. They would have never followed one so vile.

VIOLA. Ach, I am not so totally vile am I, Wood? There were moments when I thought you would follow me to Scotland if I asked. I can still claim the throne and we can make the crown our own. I wouldst make thee king, Wood. Does it tempt thee? Let the Scottish scepter be thy guide. The two of us twinned side by side.

WOOD. It would have to be side by side. (*beat*) I could never turn my back on you. Here's your prize prisoner, Fang. Scotland should reward you handsomely for her arrest.

FANG. Right you are, Wood.

VIOLA. You'll regret this, Wood. I've escaped death once before and I can do it again. I'll be back with daggers. I'll slit your throat and wash my hands in your blood.

WOOD. Careful you don't spill any on your dress.

CHARLOTTE. The spots'll never come out.

FANG. Come along, lady.

(**FANG** *escorts the struggling* **VIOLA** *a.k.a. Lady Mac-Beth out the door.*)

WOOD (*turning to* **IAGO**) And you. You go tell Quasimodo that if he's going to become king, he'll have do it without the Knights or the knife. Understand? He's going to get his any way.

IAGO. You're not as big a man as you think you are, Wood.

WOOD. Big enough to handle the likes of you. And if ever I see you in this neighborhood again, I'll sic the Venetians on you. Capiche? Now scram.

(**IAGO** *hastily scrambles out.*)

MERCUTIO. Thou hast done very well, Mr. Wood. But truthfully. Where is the Maltese Bodkin?

WOOD. Hang on, Murray.

MERCUTIO (*sighing*) Mercutio.

WOOD. Mercutio. Before I give it back, you gotta promise me that I'll never see the damn thing again.

MERCUTIO. On my word of honor. Never again shall it leave the vaults of Verona.

WOOD. Charlotte.

CHARLOTTE. Here you are. Safe and sound. (*removes the knife from her handbag and gives it to* **MERCUTIO**)

MERCUTIO. At last. I may finally return to fair Verona where the skies are always clear and they have never heard of fish and chips.

WOOD. And what'll you do then?

MERCUTIO. Discharge my vow with the knife's return. And then I shall foreswear all acts of honor. I have had my fill noble obligation and the stink of death that clings to it. My only adherence will be to pleasure and much pleasure may it bring me. Mr. Wood. Thy assistance has been invaluable. Allow me, on behalf of the Montagues and myself, to reward thee for thy services.

WOOD. I didn't do it for you. I didn't do it for the Montagues. I didn't do it for any part of Italy. I did it for

Archie. Keep your money. Spend it while you're still able to.

MERCUTIO. Nonetheless, I shall drink a toast to thee.

WOOD. Well, drink one for Archie while you're at it.

MERCUTIO. For Mr. Heath also. I salute thee Mr. Wood, for thy success. And thou, my dear, I salute thee for thy beauty and copious handbag. (*kisses her hand*)

CHARLOTTE. Oh, you charmer.

(*With a smile on his face and the knife in his hand,* **MERCUTIO** *exits.*)

WOOD (*pausing by the book on his desk*) Poor schmoe. He'll be seeing Archie in person before long.

CHARLOTTE. Bernie. How did you know the lady faked her death?

WOOD. I didn't. It was a stab in the dark. But if there's one thing I've learned it's that things aren't always what they seem. (**WOOD** *gets the bottle and a couple of glasses. He pours two drinks.*) Charlotte. I want you to join me in a drink.

CHARLOTTE. What're we drinkin' to?

WOOD. A few things. To the memory of fallen friends. To a difficult case solved. And I've made a decision.

CHARLOTTE. Yeah? What?

WOOD. We're moving. We're going to blow this burgh and move to a place we really belong.

CHARLOTTE. Yeah? Where?

WOOD. Out of England. Back to America. In fact I got a new case all lined up. (*picks up an opened letter from the desk*)

CHARLOTTE. What kinda case? Murder? Robbery?

WOOD. Nah. Just a simple divorce case. In New Orleans. There's this dame Stella Kowalski. She needs some evidence that her husband has been treating her sister bad. I figure all we got to do is get a few pictures...

(*The saxophone music fades up and over* **WOOD**'s *excited* *commentary as a beaming* **CHARLOTTE** *looks on.*)

(*CURTAIN*)

SOURCES

The action of The Maltese Bodkin draws from numerous Shakespearean plots and takes place at a number of different points in their plot lines. For instance, the play's events take place after the stories of Hamlet, Othello, MacBeth and The Tempest have concluded. Conversely it takes place before the action of Romeo and Juliet and Henry IV Part One. In addition Birnam Wood's adventure is happening concurrently with The Merchant of Venice and Richard III (despite its stated date of 1605).

The supporting characters are taken from a variety of Shakespeare's plays. The following list links the characters with their source plays:

Antonio: *The Merchant of Venice*

Viola & Sebastian: *Twelfth Night*

Iago: *Othello*

Sir John Falstaff & Mistress Nell Quickly: *Henry IV Part One, Henry IV Part Two, Henry V* and *The Merry Wives of Windsor.*

Mercutio: *Romeo and Juliet*

Puck: *A Midsummer Night's Dream*

Donalbain: *MacBeth*

Sergeant Fang: *Henry IV Part Two*

Prospero: *The Tempest*

Richard, Sir William Catesby & Sir Richard Ratcliffe: *Richard III*

Rosencrantz & Guildenstern: *Hamlet* (with a satiric dash of Tom Stoppard's *Rosencrantz and Guildenstern Are Dead*)

Also by
David Belke...

Blackpool and Parrish

Ten Times Two
The Eternal Courtship

That Darn Plot

Please visit our website **samuelfrench.com** for complete
descriptions and licensing information

GOOD BOYS
Jane Martin

A fierce encounter between fathers, one black and one white, opens a deeply disturbing chapter in their lives. The men relive the school shooting in which their sons died, one a victim and the other the shooter. When racial issues threaten to derail all hope for understanding and forgiveness, the black father's other son pushes the confrontation to a dangerous and frightening climax. This topical drama by the author of *Keely and Du* and other contemporary hits premiered at the Guthrie Theater. "Galvanizing."—*St. Paul Pioneer.* "A terrifying, terrific piece of theatre that is as memorable as it is unsettling."—*Star Tribune.* (#9935)

THE ANASTASIA TRIALS IN THE COURT OF WOMEN
Carolyn Gage

This farcical play-within-a-play is an excursion into a world of survivors and abusers. It opens as a feminist theatre group is about to put sisterhood to an iron test: each draws the role she will play on this evening from a hat. The performance that follows is the conspiracy trial of five women accused of denying Anastasia Romanov her identity. The audience votes to overrule or sustain each motion, creating a different play at every performance. "Farce, social history, debate play, agitprop, audience-participation melodrama, satire [that] makes the head reel!"—*San Diego Union-Tribune.* Wild."— *Washington Blade.* 9 f. (#3742)

See the Samuel French website at **samuelfrench.com** or our **Basic Catalogue of Plays and Musicals** for more information.

GREAT NEW COMEDIES BY KEN LUDWIG!!

LEADING LADIES

In this hilarious comedy two English Shakespearean actors, Jack and Leo, find themselves so down on their luck that they are performing "Scenes from Shakespeare" on the Moose Lodge circuit in the Amish country of Pennsylvania. When they hear that an old lady in York, PA is about to die and leave her fortune to her two long lost English nephews, they resolve to pass themselves off as her beloved relatives and get the cash. The trouble is, when they get to York, they find out that the relatives aren't nephews, but nieces! 5m, 3f (#13757)

BE MY BABY

The play tells the story of an irascible Scotsman and an up-tight English woman who are unexpectedly thrown together on the journey of a lifetime. John and Maude are brought together when his ward marries her niece. Then, when the young couple decides to adopt a new born baby, the older couple has to travel 6,000 miles to California to pick up the child and bring her safely home to Scotland. The problem is, John and Maude despise each other. To make matters worse, they get stranded in San Francisco for several weeks and are expected to jointly care for the helpless newborn. There they form a new partnership and learn some startling lessons about life and love. 3m, 3f (#04879)

See the Samuel French website at **samuelfrench.com** or our **Basic Catalogue of Plays and Musicals** for more information.

Breinigsville, PA USA
14 April 2010
236161BV00004B/2/P